Do Yourself

# No Harm

*The Secrets of Effective Prayers*

# Do Yourself

# No Harm

## *The Secrets of Effective Prayers*

**VICTOR ODUNJO**

DO YOURSELF NO HARM
**©Victor Odunjo, 2017**


Published in 2017 by
Vineyard Books Publications,
Ibadan, Nigeria.
P.O.Box 1188, Ibadan
Phone No. + 234 (0) 803 471 3765


**Contact Address**
Victor Odunjo P.O.Box 29282
Secretariat Post Office, Ibadan, Nigeria
Tel: + 234 (0) 815 681 2100, + 234 (0) 803 725 0759
E-mail: vickyshad@yahoo.co.uk


All scripture quotations are from the New King James Version
of the Bible, except otherwise stated.


**ISBN:** 978-978-32325-4-9

# PROLOGUE

In the year 1988, I read a book that literally transformed my life and practically gave me a very deep understanding of the issues we shall be discussing in this book. The book, titled *The Pastor's Wife* was written by *Sabina Wurmbrand*, the wife of the renowned and bestselling author, *Richard Wurmbrand* who was popular for his book, *Tortured for Christ* which details the account of his 14 years of torture and persecution in Communist prisons. Despite having gone home to be with the Lord, Richard and Sabina Wurmbrand left a legacy of devotion to Jesus that continues to encourage believers who come across their testimony.

A story in the book simply turned my life around early in my Christian journey. Sabina, a Jew, born and raised in present day Ukraine, and married to Richard, a Romanian Jew, gave account of a period during the Second World War. The Nazis were slaughtering Jews in their millions, but at some point, the tide began to turn against them as Stalin's men swept across Romania in 1944. One day, two Nazi soldiers were on the run for their lives and found refuge in the home of the Wurmbrands. They hid the soldiers in the basement of their apartment, rather than hand them over to the authorities. These were Jews having compassion on the killers of Jews.

For weeks, they fed them and took good care of them. You can imagine Sabina doing the dishes and laundry of the soldiers. The soldiers were dumbfounded by a couple who claimed to be Jewish Christians. Being Jews, they could have handed them over to the authorities but they refused to take vengeance. Rather, they hid them, fed them and made them comfortable. On one of those days, as Sabina went to the basement to pick up their clothes for washing, one of the soldiers, astonished to the core, decided to force a conversation with her:

> "Ma'am," he began, "We do not understand why you have decided to be so kind and generous to us and why you have refused to hand us over to the government. I surely believe the Nazis will yet again have the upper hand in this war. When that happens, I cannot assure you that I will reciprocate to you this kindness you have shown to us, because you are Jews."

Sabina's answer has rocked my world ever since. Her response can be summarized as something like this:

> "You may escape my own judgment. You may even escape the judgment of those seeking your life, but most assuredly, you will not escape the judgment of God. We won't hand you over, for my Lord said I should love my enemies and not repay evil with evil, but that does not take away the fact that God Himself will judge you if you refuse to repent."

When the tensions of war abated and the atmosphere was conducive, Sabina and her husband allowed the hardened soldiers to go. Let me ask you, would you have done the same thing?

As for me, her response to the unrepentant soldiers literally transformed me. I can still see myself right now jumping off my bed that day, running around the room and screaming at the top of my voice. I was deeply touched as I felt liberated in my spirit. It was a significant paradigm shift for me. I was sure this was the love of Christ demonstrated at its peak and I did not wish to do otherwise.

You may be wondering, what does Sabina's story have to do with prayer? That would be a valid question, although the core of her story is the locus and focus of the book you are holding. In essence, Sabina's story captures the truth of the new life we have received in Christ and the love he sheds abroad in our hearts by the Holy Ghost. God calls this life of love to be manifest in us always. Christ is glorified when, despite the opposition and challenges we face from all forms of enemies, we manifest his love, confident of the words of Scripture: "I will never leave you nor forsake you."

If Sabina's story resonates with you, then you will like Paul's too. In a Roman prison at Philippi in present-day Greece, Paul is at the corner of a prison, praying and singing hymns to God together with Silas his friend and colleague. A miracle takes place and the head of the prisons, whom Paul could consider one of his enemies in that city is about to take a tragic step. But Paul cries out with a loud voice:" *Do yourself no harm; for we are all here" (Acts 16:28)*.

There is something about Paul's response here that Sabina would have known about. Could I ask you to allow me show from the word of God how God's promise not to forsake us ought to motivate our interactions with the adversary? My hope is that we can both share in the pages that follow, the constant optic of the justice of God that makes persecuted Christians like the Wurmbrands concede vengeance to God. Let me be clear. I am not asking you to quit spiritual warfare.

I only want us to examine biblical examples of the more excellent way of love that can make confrontations by all kinds of enemies powerless.

So, what makes people like Paul and Sabina watch out for their enemies? How can we learn from them? As we learn from these Christians and from Christ himself, may our cry for those who hurt us be the same: *Do Yourself No Harm*.


**Victor Odunjo**

# ACKNOWLEDGEMENTS

The Lord gave the word and great was the company of them that published it. Each of the people who have helped to midwife this book deserves an Olympic medal.

The Holy Spirit. You do deserve more than a gold medal, but you have my heart and its sequins of gratitude. Thank you for birthing the burdens unleashed in this book. You are my source and true inspiration. Your promptings in my ears were like the Lord's words to John in Revelation: *"To the Church... write."* I appreciate the blessedness of your presence in my life.

Victoria Folasade Odunjo. Your invaluable contributions to this book qualify you as co-author and should make many a wife desire your golden heart. What a priceless editorial gift you have and a heavenly gift you have been to me. Thanks for sharing my visions and aspirations in life.

To our children, Victory, Victorian, Victor and Victoriana. Anyone would be glad to have you guys on their team. Your love is an unending song in my spirit. Now you know why nothing is more important to me.

Mrs Funsho Balepo. Your incessant prodding and patience 'wrote' this book. Every author needs editors like you. Thank you for the fantastic copy editing and many useful suggestions that make this book blush with pride.

James Yeku. What can I say? You are a writer's dream. You guys at *Textpine* should edit every book. Thank you for your invaluable editorial prowess that impacted the work greatly. I deeply appreciate your team spirit.

Reverend Ayodeji Olorunda. Sometimes busy schedules produce amazing interventions. Thank you for the beautiful foreword and for the great inspiration you are to us in God's service. We appreciate you greatly.

Thank you Victor Enioluwa Odunjo (EnnyDee), of *Leviante Technologies Ltd.*, for an excellent cover design. I am proud of your creative genius. Let's do it again very soon. And to you Bayo Adeyinka, for the kind words earlier in the process of birthing this book. To Idowu-Taylor Babatunde, for your creative inputs and support, and to *Printmarks Ventures* for the excellent work you do. Working with you has been a delight.

Pastor Olusanya and Adeola Adewusi. You provided space for the first wave of inspiration for this book. Thanks for making your abode a dwelling of the Spirit that stimulates creative germination.

And to you, the reader. Thanks for the privilege of your time. Please forgive me if, as you read, my words keep taking you to the Bible. That Berean inclination is to your credit.

# FOREWORD

This book in your hands, *DO YOURSELF NO HARM*, will provoke you no matter where you are at in your Christian journey, and there are not many like it around anymore, so do not put it away. Your journey will be the better for it if you continue to read it no matter how much it challenges what you have held dear for such a long time. Having read it myself, I know it is a mighty privilege to write this foreword, and I am grateful for the opportunity.

*DO YOURSELF NO HARM* chronicles an imagined journal of Paul the Apostle, gleaned from Scriptures to unravel the heart of this exemplary leader of the Modern Church. The aim is to reveal his desire to see the Lord glorified in the lives of even his most fierce enemies. It uses the great story in Acts 16 as a springboard to pass across an essential message to the current dispensation of believers. The book appears to take away the crutches of those whose stance and desire is to see their enemies perish through *"fall- down-and-die-prayers"* as the author so succinctly describes it. If that is where you are at in your journey currently, you may want to turn the book over and walk away, but, please, do not!

In Chapters 7 and 8, the author, rather than offering crutches, carefully and graciously gives back a compass to locate the right enemy in your daily battles, a weapon to engage that enemy successfully every time and a solid ground from which to fight battles you can never lose. I promise you my friend; it would be exhilarating when you get there. Let me also advise you to resist the temptation to flip to the closing stages to read that first. As someone who used to do this when reading detective novels in the days of yore, I can tell you that you would have lost the context and therefore the benefit of the transformation that is possible and intended.

Have you ever wondered why the Apostle Paul told the Jailor, "Do yourself No Harm, for we are all here"? I strongly believe that he did for three reasons. First is that in the particular earthquake that came to the prison, God was there. Indeed, He came to inhabit the praises of His people. Second, Paul and Silas knew that the only place to be is where God is, even if it were a prison! Third, they knew if the Lord were with them, they had no enemy to fear because He is the Almighty, Jehovah, and the Man of War.

These are the truths and more contained in and expressed by the book *Do Yourself No Harm;* that the battle is not yours, ultimately; your battle is God's, and He knows how to fight for you, my friend, converting enemies to enablers!

**AYODEJI OLORUNDA**
(A Practicing Consultant Architect called to Pastor
THE LATTER HOUSE, Ibadan, Nigeria)

# CONTENT

# DO YOURSELF NO HARM:
# A DAY IN PAUL'S DIARY I

Today is an unforgettable day for Paul and Silas. Being a scholar, Paul probably kept a diary. From his words to Timothy about his parchments and writing materials, we know that documenting his missionary efforts mattered to him. I am sure you have read his epistles, but would it not be nice to uncover the likely contents of his diary too? In the next two chapters, I hope to introduce a reconstruction of his diary entries, which explain and expose a few episodes of his dramatic life. God orchestrated this special day and made sure the events that took place at Philippi were written for our admonition. The lessons here should make us think again about the way we respond to those who hurt us. They set a great example and teach what it means to love all men and to choose to pray the right kind of prayers.

### *Entry I: The Prison Quake*
### *Location: Philippi*
### *Time: 02:00*

**The ground under you had just convulsed in a lone prison-quake.**

If I saw you just about to harm yourself, should I leave you to?

Oh yes! You offended me. You messed me up. You laid heavy lashes on my back. I bled.

You then threw me into jail, judged me guilty without trial, denied me freedom. However now, because of me, you are about to harm yourself, should I leave you to such fatal act?

Mr. Jailer, you suddenly awoke from a deep slumber. The ground under you had just convulsed in a lone prison- quake. Like a cat, you sprang up to your feet, the instincts of military training getting the better of you.

As an artful dodger, you prowled around, pacing frantically as you surveyed the prison facility, sword drawn in hand.

To your chagrin, all the prison doors were wide open. You are incensed. What the hell could have happened here? How? More fear and terror seized you.

Instantly the thoughts of what this meant to your life and career rushed through your keen mind. There has been a prison-break! And the inevitable has happened. All prisoners have escaped.

————❧———— That, you were too sure had happened.

**Being a gallant soldier yourself, rather than face a cruel, painful and humiliating public execution, you chose to go down honourably... quietly... privately...**

————❧————

What criminal worth his salt would see the prison doors wide open and remain inside?

But I am no criminal! I am a harmless servant of the Most High God.

You thought I had escaped. You were wrong.

You knew the consequences of a jail-break and what the Jury's verdict would surely be.

It's life for life, your life in exchange for the lives of escaped prisoners. The Roman authorities made sure every prison head faces this: a cruel, painful death in the hands of heartless executioners.

Simon Peter's lone jail- break in Jerusalem a few months ago remains very fresh on your mind. Your friend, the jailer, paid the supreme price for that lone escape (Acts 12:19).

Being a gallant soldier yourself, rather than face a cruel, painful and humiliating public execution, you chose to go down honourably... quietly... privately...

So you drew your sword, ready to fall on it, hasty to end it all.

As I watch your silent drama from the corner of the prison cell, what should I do?

*And the keeper of the prison, awaking from sleep and seeing the prison doors open, supposing the prisoners had fled, drew his sword and was about to kill himself. But Paul called with a loud voice, saying, "Do yourself no harm, for we are all here"* (Acts 16: 27-28).

With eyes fully accustomed to the darkness, I saw you from afar as you lifted the sword. From my dark cell, I heard your words as you hurriedly said your last prayers.

What should I do?

You thought we had escaped, I knew we had not.

Shouldn't I have said to myself, *'Go ahead and kill yourself, serves you right, you sure deserve to die. Lord, thank you for avenging your anointed'?*

Or should I reach out to you in love and cry, *'hey! Don't do that to yourself. We went nowhere'?*

Well, I chose the latter. I screamed at the top of my voice, *'Man! Do yourself no harm, for we are all here.'*

Rather than allow you die, I chose to let you live. Rather than rejoice as you spilled your own blood, I reached out to you in love. No matter what you did to me, I would rather have you saved than have you spend eternity in hell.

For your hatred, you will get love. For your wickedness, goodness. Only goodness, in return.

Yes, for persecuting me, you deserve my prayers, my blessings, and my goodness. For my Lord has clearly instructed me:

*"...LOVE your enemies, BLESS those who curse you, DO GOO D to those who hate you, and PRAY for those who spitefully use you and persecute you"*
*(Matt 5:44).*

That will always be my stand. Forever!

And I am aware of the Torah and the Psalms, for Gamaliel was my teacher. I know David's words: *"My eye shall see my desire on mine enemies and mine ears shall hear my desire of the wicked that rise up against me"* *(Ps 92:11 KJV).*

Oh yes! David said this and much more. We are on the same page, for I also wish my ears to hear my desire on the wicked that rise against me.

Although, I have another kind of desire for them. A desire birthed by the Spirit of Christ.

"My one and only desire for the wicked that rise up against me is that they might come to the saving knowledge of my Saviour. I want them bow to His Lordship, love Him and serve Him."

This is how the beloved physician Luke recalled this account in his history books:

*But Paul called with a loud voice saying, "Do yourself no harm, for we are all here."*

*Then he (the Jailer) called for a light, ran in, and fell down trembling before Paul and Silas. And he brought them out and said, "Sirs, what must I do to be saved?" So they said, "Believe on the Lord Jesus Christ, and you will be saved, you and your household."*

*Then they spoke the word of the Lord to him and to all who were in his house.*

*And he took them the same hour of the night and washed their stripes. And immediately he and all his family were baptized. Now when he had brought them into his house, he set food before them; and he rejoiced, having believed in God with all his household (Acts 16:28-34).*

He and his household? What a glorious dramatic twist to a great night! What a God!

I had a choice to allow him *"fall down and die[1]"* on his sword, but I chose the way of love and it worked. Love always wins. God has taught me to overcome evil with good.

So, let me restate my desire for my enemies: I want to see them submit to the Lord, love Him and glorify Him on the earth.

---

[1] Fall-down- and-die prayers in the Nigerian church are the typical spiritual warfare petitions that are targeted at enemies. Whether these enemies are real people or demons is often lost on those who pray these prayers. Aside from Fall-down-and-die, similar other expressions used throughout this book include: "operation-no-mercy-somersault-and-die-by- fire-by force"by-fire-by force, die by fire, etc.

Last night, the jailer was my tormentor. Today, I am his mentor.

The night before, I lay prostrate before him as he laid heavy lashes on my back.

Today, he lay prostrate before me as he trembled and cried out to my God.

The wounds he created, he gladly washed and bandaged.

In one night, my jailer turned full circle: he passed from death to life.

How am I so sure this change is real? Of course, I am.

Here is the test: *We know that we have passed from death to life, because we love the brethren... (1 John 3:14).*

Last night, he was overzealously cruel towards me. Today, he sets a table before me.

Why then should he *"somersault and die"* when God has designed to use my enemy to set a table before me?

My enemies today may have been ordained by God to be my destiny helpers tomorrow.

*Oh, the depth of the riches both of the wisdom and knowledge of God!*

*How unsearchable are His judgments and His ways past finding out! (Rom. 11:33).*

What a God! What a way! What a life!

Chapter

# DO YOURSELF NO HARM:
# A DAY IN PAUL'S DIARY II

The joy of salvation overwhelms me as I think of what to make out of Paul's story and this jailer. I probably can conclude Paul also experienced such joy; he experienced the thrill of seeing somebody who had no inheritance in Christ surrender to Him. Indeed, an enemy who could have been told in prayer to *"fall down and die"* has rather fallen into the grace and salvation of God because Paul heeded the words of Christ that we love and pray for our enemies. When such enemies eventually bow to the God of heaven, it provokes gratitude in the heart of believers who are excited to witness an expansion in the kingdom of God. I imagine a good way to conclude my reconstruction of his diary is to reflect on his gratitude to God's saving grace. You may also have noted yourself that Paul's presence at the stoning of Stephen helped him greatly. I also unpack this a little, with the words of Peter in mind: *'For to this you were*

9

*called, because Christ also suffered for us, leaving us an example, that you should follow His steps: "Who committed no sin, nor was deceit found in His mouth", Who, when He was reviled, did not revile in return; when He suffered, He did not threaten, but committed Himself to Him who judges righteously' (1 Pet 2:21-23).* May the Lord find us faithful as he did Stephen and Paul.

**Entry II: Gratitude**

**Location: Philippi**

**Time: 11:00**

Dear Lord, your ways are mysterious and pass finding out.

Thank you for granting me the grace to extend to others what grace and mercies you extended to me.

If you marked iniquity, Lord, would I stand?

I was the chief of sinners, plotting cruel and evil schemes against your people.

Was I not the ring leader in the cruel execution of that great soul called Stephen? Great man. Gallant soldier of the cross.

From his mouth I first heard the truth of your gospel explicitly preached. Quite piercing, the truth from his heart spoke to mine. I could not stand it, for it meant a total collapse of all my glory in self-righteousness.

I was too blinded by the traditions of my fathers to heed the wisdom of truth. I therefore determined that Stephen must die.

Too civilized to cast the first stone, I incited the mob against him, arguing blindly in defense of the law. I gave the marching orders and the mob went berserk. They became violent and pelted Stephen with heavy stones. I shouted the more, calling for his blood. I helped them with their clothes as they strove to outdo one another in this bizarre act (Acts7:58).

> **Too civilized to cast the first stone, I incited the mob against him, arguing blindly in defense of the law.**

Beloved Stephen, on account of me and at my orders, was wasted, judged guilty without trial.

What kind of prayer should Stephen say to you concerning us?

Pray for us or pray against us?

Lord, even as I write this, I shudder.

Wouldn't he be justified to bring a curse on us, even to our fourth generation as we took his life? He could have prayed:

*"Lord, avenge me of my enemies. Require my blood from their hands. Let their families know only bloodshed. May their children fall down and die mysteriously. For they have touched me, the anointed of the Lord."*

No. Stephen said no such thing: for if he did, I may not be writing this now. With his bloodied face, Stephen looked up into heaven, and with his last breath he cried:

*"Lord, lay not this sin to their charge."*

*And he kneeled down, and cried with a loud voice 'Lord lay not this sin to their charge'. And when he has said this, he fell asleep (Acts 7:60 KJV).*

What? I heard him and was shocked to the marrow. Rather than curse us to hell, he received forgiveness for us.

As we took his life away, he gave us life in return. Did I not deserve the curse? Yet he prayed for me as he departed.

I cut his life short, yet he regarded me not as his enemy.

His sole desire for me, this arch-enemy of the gospel, was that I come to truly know the God of my fathers, and Jesus Christ, whom He sent to die for me.

**As we took his life away, he gave us life in return.**

What a man! What a rare disciple of yours.

Dear Lord, Stephen chose to walk in your footsteps, choosing to be like you.

The elders in Jerusalem and the other witnesses told us!

That as the nails were driven into your palms on that dark day at Golgotha, in your anguish, you looked into the eyes of those who drove the nails in and prayed:

*"Father, forgive them, for they do not know what they do" (Luke 23:34).*

Stephen did exactly what you did.

You both forgave your enemies while they cut short your existence. You both resisted unto blood striving against vengeance.

> **You both forgave your enemies while they cut short your existence. You both resisted unto blood striving against vengeance.**

Dear Lord, thank you for honouring Stephen's prayer for me.

In mercy, you encountered me on Damascus road. You had mercy on me, your Persecutor-in- Chief.

Oh, what a day!

On my way to Damascus, I saw this blinding flash of light, greater than and separate from the light of the sun, which truly blinded me. The impact of it flung me off the horse I rode, and in a jiffy, I was rolling dangerously in the desert dust.

Still reeling from shock and disbelief, I heard you call my name: *"Saul, Saul, why persecutest thou me?"*

Who? Me? Persecuting you? I wasn't persecuting God!

No one in his right mind would.

I was persecuting men: heady men, senseless, narrow-minded religious bigots.

So I thought.

Unknown to me, fighting your people meant contending with you.

And when in defiance I asked who was speaking to me, you sternly warned; *"I am Jesus whom thou persecutest. It is hard for thee to kick against the pricks."*

> you admonished me: Saul, do yourself no harm. It's dangerous for you to fight against me.

That did it for me. Lord, you admonished me: *Saul, do yourself no harm. It's dangerous for you to fight against me.*

Like the jailer, I bowed to your Lordship and cried *Lord, what wilt thou have me to do?*

Today, I am glad I have also walked in your footsteps.

What you gave to your 'nailers,' I gave to my jailer.

I blessed rather than curse, and sons were brought unto glory.

Lord, you've brought this message back to me afresh today: that only *love* ultimately wins.

To your prayer, *Father forgive them* came the response from the Centurion present at Golgotha: *"Truly, this was the Son of God"*

To Stephen's prayer, *Lord, lay not this sin to their charge* came my response: *Lord, what would thou have me to do?*

And to my cry, *Do yourself no harm* came my jailer's response: *Sirs, what must I do to be saved?*

Love seems to always carry the day.

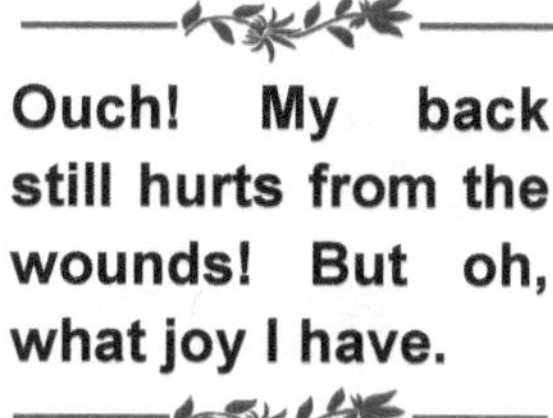


Lord, I have a fresh understanding of your workings again today: that the way of love is still the most excellent way. Thank you for enabling me to walk again in this truth.

*Ouch!* My back still hurts from the wounds! But oh, what joy I have.

My stripes and sufferings are not always in vain, so I glory in them. That's when your power rests on me the more. When I am weak, then am I truly strong.

Lord, it's time to catch some sleep, but not until I have prayed this one prayer you seem to be laying on my heart:

*Dear Lord, may the upcoming generations of your children learn this great truth and follow your footsteps as we did. May they not reverse this truth or stand it on its head by selfish and anxiety-laden prayers or conduct. For your Spirit speaks expressly to me that in the last days, men shall be lovers of themselves and become haters of men.*

*Rather than show your love and sincerely pray for their perceived or real human enemies for whom*

*Christ died, they will curse and pray for their physical harm and seek their spiritual and eternal destruction. We have not so learned this of you, Lord. I perceive by your Spirit that false and erroneous teachings shall emerge, breeding much hatred in your body towards perceived and real enemies, both within and outside the church.*

**Dear Lord, may the upcoming generations of your children learn this great truth and follow your footsteps as we did.**

*Yes, many leaders shall also champion these errors, thereby multiplying hatred, animosity and confusion in the world. Lord, let the truth dawn on them: that the Son of Man came not to destroy men's lives but to save them. And your children are not agents of destruction, but of peace, of love, of salvation. Remind them, Lord, that we wrestle not with humans, not against flesh and blood; that men are not the real enemies; that the demonic spiritual forces working in and through them are the true culprits. Open their eyes, Lord, in the last days to know who their true enemies really are- the principalities and powers- and to aim their weapons of warfare at these wicked spirits, lest they fight as they that beat the air. Then, and only then can your gospel truly fill the earth with great impact, as the waters cover the sea. This I pray in*

*the name before whom every knee shall bow, the Name of Jesus. Amen.*

How refreshing!

Now I can say like King David:

*I will both lie down in peace, and sleep: for You alone, O LORD, make me dwell in safety (Ps. 4:8).*

3

# THOU SHALL NOT KILL

If Paul was a contemporary of ours, how would our society receive the news that he forgave a man who persecuted him? Would they have thought he should not have been kind and merciful? How about you? How would you relate with the two Nazi soldiers who hurt and killed your relatives? I am sure, like Sabina, you have got to a point in your walk with God in which judgment over another human life is deferred to God. I believe Paul and, particularly Sabina, teach us something about the important commandment God gave to Moses. When God says you must not take another person's life, my sense of this is that he is saying, "Since you have no power to create life, you should not indiscriminately take it. Do not become a judge over what you cannot master or create." I will be addressing these issues in this chapter, trusting that we can both unravel God's truth from the Bible. Many Christians, I believe, do not have any issue with this sacred injunction. But is it possible that a new generation of Christians not well instructed in the word of God do not see any harm in killing other humans in prayers? Yes, it sounds bizarre but that appears to be the new religion in town.

**It's the prayer point that makes even the weak and lazy receive sudden burst of energy to pray.**

**The deep sleeper becomes wide awake to join the frenzy of shouts around him.**

It is a new wave among God's children, particularly in the Nigerian church, a foremost evangelical force in the comity of nations.

There is a new rave, a new genre of spirituality expressed through prayer in our prayer meetings and at our prayer altars. Whole sessions of all-night vigils are dedicated to it.

Volumes of books have been written on it that turned bestsellers.

Countless sermons have been preached on it.

It's the prayer point that makes even the weak and lazy receive sudden burst of energy to pray.

The deep sleeper becomes wide awake to join the frenzy of shouts around him.

Ministries have been built around its theme.

Advertisement on it attracts crowds to the Prayer Mountains more than prayers for dying souls will ever do.

Yet it calls for a critical examination in the light of scriptures, and the life to which we have been called unto in Christ Jesus.

This genre of prayer is popularly referred to as ***Judgmental Prayers.***

It is fervent prayer geared to seeking the destruction, death and sometimes the eternal annihilation of so-called enemies, real, imagined or perceived.

It is the art of raining curses in prayer on human beings who have offended us; men and women for whom Christ died.

> **It is the art of raining curses in prayer on human beings who have offended us; men and women for whom Christ died.**

Some tagged this prayer culture *Operation No Mercy*, forgetting that the scriptures teach that "Blessed are the merciful."

Like Jonah reminds us, these people, turning to the services of false idols, diviners and herbalists, have forsaken their own mercy (2:8). People forget to be merciful when God ceases to be the focus of their lives. People no longer seek to be God's channel of mercy to others. All they need do now, as a matter of fact, is find their way to some churches and prayer mountains, where they are assured that the "God" of heaven will do a far better job than herbalists in judging their enemies for them.

**the most fervent prayers He hears are for the destruction of the same harvest.**

We had also thought that, at best, this kind of prayers were the exclusive preserve of certain denominations not focused on Christ, but now, mainstream, born-again, tongue-talking, Pentecostal and evangelical Christians have developed their own patents which, sadly, have been exported the world over.

In the process, God's altar has been desecrated with polluted prayer offerings and His image as the God of Love has plummeted. Many now see him primarily as the god that would rather rain down thunder.

While God waits for His children to cry unto Him, the Lord of the harvest, for the deliverance and salvation of men from the clutches of sin and Satan, the most fervent prayers He hears are for the destruction of the same harvest.

Simply put, those who pray these imprecatory prayers are men and women who forget to be merciful, having received mercy themselves. No wonder Jesus said, *The Harvest truly is plenteous, but the labourers are few.*

Few there are who want the Lord of the Harvest to save. Many more wouldn't mind the harvest set ablaze with the fire of hell because of their selfish interests. They see men like trees.

The essence of this book is to reveal the mind of God on the crucial issues of spiritual warfare, thereby setting the people of God free. The Bible succinctly puts it: My people perish for lack of knowledge (Hosea 4:6).

Many pray these prayers, not knowing the position of God's word about such topics. They simply follow the crowd. But when we know the truth, it sets us free.

We will do ourselves a lot of good if we channel our energy to pray according to the will of God. Many simply don't study the word themselves, thus allowing people to mislead them by using isolated scriptural verses to say what God has not said.

**We will do ourselves a lot of good if we channel our energy to pray according to the will of God.**

Are the days of the Berean Christians clean gone forever? When men studied scriptures themselves to see if the things they were taught were truly so, regardless of the caliber of those who taught them.

When I consider the subject of biblical literacy and this vital need to search the scriptures for ourselves, this verse about the Bereans always fascinates me: *These were more noble than those in Thessalonica, in that they received the word with all readiness of mind, and SEARCHED THE SCRIPTURES DAILY whether these things were so (Acts17:11KJV, emphasis mine).*

Who was the preacher of the word that the Berean Christians sought to verify and re-appraise daily here? The preacher is no other than Brother Paul, the veteran Doctor of Law, the Hebrew of Hebrews.

> *But when the Jews from Thessalonica learned that the word of God was preached by Paul at Berea...*
> *(Acts 17:13).*

**If Paul's messages needed to be judged and verified for accuracy and consistency with the teaching of Christ, who are the Apostles and Bishops of our day whose words we consider infallible or above error and require no verification?**

If Paul's messages needed to be judged and verified for accuracy and consistency with the teaching of Christ, who are the Apostles and Bishops of our day whose words we consider infallible or above error and require no verification?

Let's be wise. Like the Berean Christians, let's be noble and diligent. Let's learn to search the scriptures by ourselves, for ourselves to verify every word we are taught, regardless of who taught it, lest deception and error sway us in a wrong direction.

It is with this open mind that I want us to go together to see what God says in His word concerning the issue of judgmental prayers.

# Thou Shall Not Kill

The Word of God categorically states, "Thou shall not kill." This is the sixth commandment of the popular Ten Commandments.

Is this commandment outdated? Or did it expire with the law? Can Christians now kill in the New Testament?

**The 7th commandment says: *Thou shall not commit adultery* (Exo. 20:13). Today, as Christians, we still should not commit adultery.**

I know you agree with me that this commandment of God is not done away with in Christ. In fact, while the many ceremonial laws of Moses have been done away with in Christ, not a single command of the Ten Commandments is irrelevant today.

The 7th commandment says: Thou shall not commit adultery (Exo. 20:13). Today, as Christians, we still should not commit adultery.

The 8th commandment says: Thou shall not steal (Exo 20:16). Can we now steal as Christians? Are we free to bear false witness? Should we fail to honour our fathers and mothers? The answer is No.

To the Christian, therefore, God says: "Thou shall not kill". A Christian who kills is a murderer. No murderer will inherit the kingdom of God (Rev 21:8). In the Old Testament which operated "an eye for an eye" policy, a murderer would be killed too.

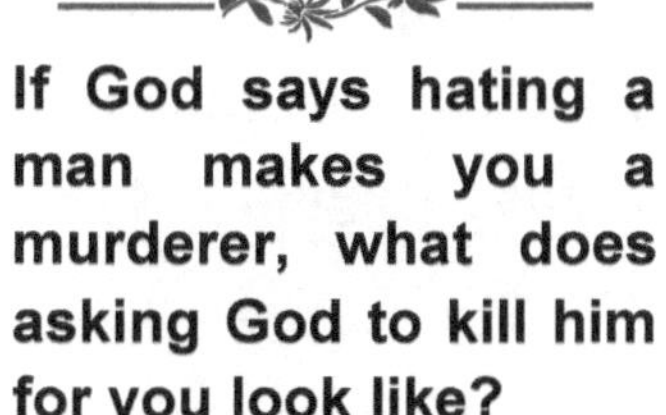
**If God says hating a man makes you a murderer, what does asking God to kill him for you look like?**

When Christ came, the bar was raised. You are a murderer not only when you kill, you are equally one when you hate a fellow brother. Now we can fully appreciate John's words:

*Whoever hates his brother is a murderer, and you know that no murderer has eternal life abiding in him*

*(1 John 3:15).*

If God says hating a man makes you a murderer, what does asking God to kill him for you look like? How then did we come about these *fall down and die* prayers? Just how did we get to this point?

If you pray that someone, anyone, should fall down and die, and he does, what should we call you? A saint? A murderer of course. Who killed him? You did. It's murder, first degree murder.

Like people do when they take the names of their enemies to spiritualists, you brought a name to the place of prayer, to the church, asking God for his demise. Even if he does not die, ordinarily bringing his name before God to be killed makes you guilty of attempted murder which is punishable by law in our secular world, if found guilty. Even in the secular world, if intent to murder is established, a man is equally guilty.

**Little wonder God does not answer such prayers. To pray that a human being should die is to pray amiss.**

The word of God has not changed. No murderer will inherit the kingdom of God (Rev 21:8).

Little wonder God does not answer such prayers. To pray that a human being should die is to pray amiss.

Since you began to pray these judgmental prayers, how many of those enemies have fallen and died? How many can you count on your fingers? The answer is simple: God simply refuses to answer these prayers.

God, more often than not, would rather turn around the situation that warranted the prayer in the first place, without eliminating the person. This was what we gleaned from the account of Paul's journal entries.

Look again at the story of the jailer discussed in Paul's journal. If God wanted the Jailer dead, couldn't the earthquake have killed him?

You had better thank God for not answering those prayers the way you prayed them, lest you have blood on your hands by now. Considering this, we urgently need to stop asking evil to befall our supposed enemies. To pray for them that persecute you and despitefully use you is what the Lord instructs us to do, not to pray that they die. What for? You cannot give life. Stop asking God to take it. Let it be the prerogative of the life- giver only to take life. God says...*Avenge not yourselves...vengeance is mine... (Rom. 12:19)*. Let the life-giving King decide when and how to repay. That is what is expected of us as new creation in Christ Jesus.

## Judgmental Prayers in the Old Testament

More often than not, people justify these prayers with quotes from the Old Testament. They imagine that since saints of old like David prayed these prayers and God recorded them for us to read, such petitions must be vital. The truth, without belabouring this matter, is that Jesus has come as a fulfillment of the law, putting it aside because it was fraught with imperfection. He then gave us a new life, a new way and established new kingdom principles. To practise the old in its raw form would be at cross purposes with God's eternal counsel which He has re-established in Christ Jesus His Son.

Look at these scriptures:

> *God who at various times and in various ways spoke in time past to the fathers by the prophets has in these last days spoken to us by His Son, whom he hath appointed heir of all things, through whom also He made the worlds. (Heb. 1:1-2).*

> *But now, he (Christ) has obtained a more excellent ministry, in as much as He is also a mediator of a*

*better covenant, which was established on better promises.* ***For if that first covenant had been faultless, then no place would have been sought for a second.*** *Because finding fault with them, He says, Behold the days are coming, says the LORD when I will make a new covenant with the house of Israel and the house of Judah*

*(Heb.8:6-8, emphasis mine).*

**In the Beatitudes, Jesus recalled what was in the law, and what now shall be, going forward.**

God has spoken with finality by His Son, thereby putting away the old with its frailty and errors. In the Beatitudes, Jesus recalled what was in the law, and what now shall be, going forward. He put away the old to establish the new.

Hebrews 8:13 puts it succinctly: *"In that He says: 'A new covenant', he has made the first obsolete. Now what is becoming obsolete and growing old is ready to vanish away."*

We shall dwell more on this in the next chapter.

Suffice it to say now that in the light of the above scriptures, it simply means there are prayers in the Old Testament you cannot pray justifiably as a New Testament saint.

# God Sees Differently

I will say it again: It is criminal, spiritually callous to pray that your supposed enemy should die and perish. It is jungle justice in the realm of the spirit. Don't judge people guilty of capital punishment without trial. You are not the judge. Only the righteous judge- the all-knowing God- should determine that. The life-giver alone should have the prerogative to take it.

**It is criminal, spiritually callous to pray that your supposed enemy should die and perish. It is jungle justice in the realm of the Spirit. Don't judge people guilty of capital punishment without trial. You are not the judge.**

Like I earlier said, God hardly ever answers such prayers. You know why? *God does not see as man sees. Man looks at the outward appearance; God alone sees the heart* (See 1 Sam 16:7).

The many people we tag today as enemies and we pray to die are not seen so by God. In many cases, our evil hearts, lusts and selfish desires make us tag men as enemies. As a matter of fact, some supposed "enemies" are instruments in God's hands to reveal to us our lusts, selfish desires, and evil hearts.

To consider this point a little more, let us explore some scenarios. My first example is from the Bible.

## Scenario 1

In the book of 1 Kings 21, we have an interesting and relevant account that explains this lesson. King Ahab approached a neighbour, Naboth, asking for permission to annex Naboth's land because of the proximity to his palace. Ahab readily offered to pay a generous amount for it, or better still, exchange it for lands in other choice areas in the city. According to him, he wants to make of it a vegetable farm (planting temporary crop) even though the original owner planted vines (permanent crop).

Naboth politely refused the offer, citing family tradition as his main reason for turning down a juicier offer from His Excellency, the king. *It's the inheritance of my fathers, our pride for many generations, now passed down to me, for which I also hope to pass to my children,* he seemed to say. Is this not clear enough and tenable? Yes, but greedy and covetous Ahab would not take "no" for an answer. He went home sulking, lost appetite for food and sleep over another man's property.

While he could do whatever he liked with his many property scattered in highbrow areas across the land, nothing would suffice until he annexes a poor subject's land, not minding destroying age-long, enviable family tradition in the process. The land must be taken by fire by force. Thus, Naboth became the king's enemy that must fall down and die. This story is not particularly my focus. I just think it has some points that are relevant to this topic.

The question is: *Was Naboth truly an enemy that deserved to die in this circumstance? What exactly did he do wrong?* Well, he did *offend* someone. He was standing in the way of the greed of a heartless royal couple and so must be outright eliminated to satisfy their lusts. A well perfected conspiracy worked as orchestrated by Jezebel, the wife. Naboth was successfully eliminated. He fell down and died. He died a painful cruel death for doing nothing wrong other than exercise his fundamental human right—the freedom to sell or not to sell his own property.

> **Naboth was not only stoned to death by the royal decree of greed, he also had no decent burial. Dogs ate his corpse. He became a victim of high-level politics**

Naboth was not only stoned to death by the royal decree of greed, he also had no decent burial. Dogs ate his corpse. He became a victim of high-level politics, for refusing to sell his birth right. It was a grand conspiracy and the plot was successfully executed.

This scenario plays out daily in our contemporary world. Outsiders may not know the true story. In the time of old, murderers don't go unpunished: He who kills by the sword perishes by it. Through Prophet Elijah, the Almighty God Himself gave the verdict on both Ahab and Jezebel his wife who orchestrated the plot: *Have you murdered and also taken possession?... In the place where dogs licked the blood of Naboth, dogs shall lick your blood, even yours... the dogs shall eat Jezebel by the wall of Jezreel (1 Kings 21:19, 23).*

More deadly curses were pronounced on Ahab's lineage. It was blood for blood. God paid them back in their own coins. They also had no decent burial.

Did you realise Ahab did not kill Naboth himself? He used vagabonds and street urchins, those we call *area boys* in

Lagos to carry out the job. But he was the one God judged primarily, not the instruments that were used. The same way many want to use "God" to kill their supposed "enemies", making God an accomplice in their crime.

In the same way Ahab used vagabonds, Christians want to use God. He will not be a partaker in such act of cruelty. He cannot be tempted with evil neither does he tempt any man. They had better approach herbalists who don't care where the truth lies.

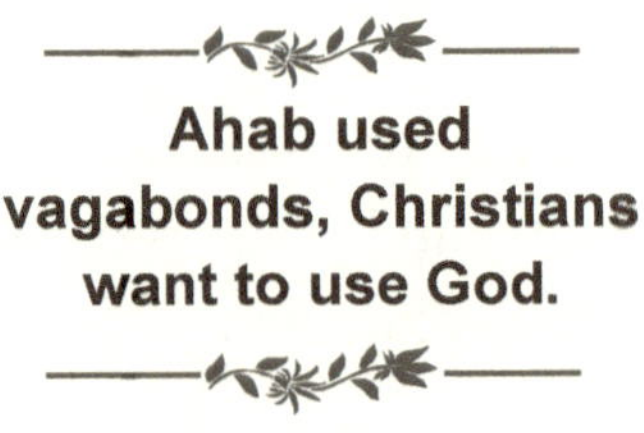

**Ahab used vagabonds, Christians want to use God.**

Can you now see why it was in your own interest God did not answer your judgmental prayers? You would have had to be judged like Ahab was, if your motives were wrong.

The truth is, it is for such flimsy issues that a lot of us want our supposed enemies to die. People are that petty and most people we tag enemies are not one at all. And if they truly are, a mature Christian leaves God to judge them Himself. We amass *enemies* for the wrong reasons. Even in the Ahab story, as soon as he saw Prophet Elijah approaching him, Ahab exclaimed *"Have you found me, O my enemy?"* (See 1Kings 21:20). In Ahab's crooked mind, anyone who boldly stands to speak truth to him is also an enemy that must be crushed. What a world!

## Scenario 2

As an official in the Nigerian banking system for about two decades, I witnessed various scenarios while managing different categories of customers and their banking activities. One of such situations is instructive.

You approach a wealthy businessman or a relative for financial assistance. The person politely declines, saying he is not able to help at that moment. *That's a big lie,* you reasoned. *With his fleet of cars, houses and all his children schooling abroad, how would he not have the common Twenty Thousand Naira I am asking for?*

For not helping, he begins to take on the status of an enemy in your mind. You reason further: *He does not want my 'progress' in life. That's why he has refused to help. He can go to blazes with his money.*

You may even start to call him names.

The day a prayer point is raised against those who want to hinder your progress in life, his name begins to pop up, but, in reality, he has done you no harm.

Unknown to you, he truly might not have been able to help then. In the course of my career, I met seemingly great men, big names, whose businesses were at the mercies of bank loans and overdrafts. Even when their account balances read *Ten Million Naira,* they couldn't afford the luxury of spending a naira out of it on themselves, much less giving to anyone. They may have issued out third-party cheques against those funds to reputable business partners, and the bank instruments must never be returned or they would lose credibility, never able to continue in their business. They are always under pressure, asking their Bank Managers to ensure the cheques are not returned under any circumstance. They have their creditors breathing down their necks; they are at the risk of losing all and forfeiting their collateral to banks in the event of default.

Imagine that you approach such a business man at such times they have much on their plate. They may simply decline to help. Some just can't take any additional pressure on their finances. Why would anyone classify such a person as an enemy? If you pray against such, you pray amiss. God, the righteous judge will not hear you. You had better go to some spiritualist. Only Satan can help you kill your enemies regardless of where the truth lies, like he did for Ahab in Naboth's case. He is the master of confusion and evil.

You see, things don't always seem as they appear. No wonder the Lord instructs us to "not *judge according to appearance, but judge righteous judgment*" (John 7:24).

Even if a man has the means, but refuses to help, how does that make him an enemy? It's his money, and he chooses what he does with it. Should a child of God lose sleep or appetite over that?

How would you feel when you are stuck in a Lagos traffic and a beggar approaches you for alms? You sure have alms but just not in the mood to give one. The beggar is also certain you have but have refused to give.

> **Why would anyone classify such a person as an enemy? If you pray against such, you pray amiss. God, the righteous judge will not hear you.**

If, for your refusal, he decides to smash your side mirror and takes to his heels, how would you feel? Should that be a grievous offense? Do you owe the beggar alms? It is the same when you make an enemy out of someone who has what you need, but has refused to help.

Look unto God alone and do yourself no harm. Rather than keep malice, expecting God to punish innocent people who did you no wrong, let it go and wish them well. That should be the spirit. And your Father in heaven will make His own way for you. In any case, you are better off putting your trust in God.

## Scenario 3

A man once came to Jesus with a passionate request that seemed to require the urgent attention of God.

> *Then someone called from the crowd, 'Teacher, please tell my brother to divide our father's estate with me'*

> *(Luke 12:13, N LT).*

Jesus' response was shocking.

*"Jesus replied, 'Friend, who made me a judge over you to decide such things as that?'"*
*(Luke 12:14, N LT).*

**The man prayed amiss and Jesus refused to answer him.**

In other words, the Lord is saying, *don't insult me. Don't drag me into petty selfish matters. That is not why I am here.*

The man prayed amiss and Jesus refused to answer him. In the Lord's next statement, we read: *beware of covetousness,* an indirect way of saying the man was covetous because Jesus knew the motive behind his request.

Of course, our Lord is a mediator and Judge. He is the mediator between God and man (1 Tim 2:6) and the Judge of all the earth. But He cannot allow Himself to be used to fester our greed and selfishness, as most judgmental prayers portray.

## Scenario 4

When we judge others, we sometimes condemn ourselves. And this leads me to the final scenario.

*Therefore, you are inexcusable, O man, whoever you are who judge, for in whatever you judge another you condemn yourself; for you who judge practice the same things...And do you think this, O man, you who judge those practicing such things, and doing the same, that you will escape the judgment of God?" (Rom 2; 1, 3).*

A lot of the people who seek the death penalty from God for their enemies are themselves deserving of same: And whatever makes God kill their supposed enemies will, for fairness, turn Him against them also.

Think of this: A man fervently prays to God to get rid of his "enemy", possibly a boss at work who unjustifiably hinders his promotion for years; but then he himself is an adulterer, committing adultery with other

> A lot of the people who seek the death penalty from God for their enemies are themselves deserving of same:

men's wives with reckless abandon. How come he has the audacity to approach God to destroy his boss when he himself is an enemy of God?

> *Adulterers and adulteresses! Do you not know that friendship with the world is enmity with God? Whoever therefore wants to be a friend of the world makes himself an enemy of God*
>
> *(James 4:4).*

> How come he has the audacity to approach God to destroy his boss when he himself is an enemy of God?

How does it sound to you? An enemy of God who himself is deserving of death before God now wishes God to overlook his own sins and mete out judgment on another, for his own selfish sake. It doesn't work that way. *When a man comes to equity, he comes with clean hands,* the popular maxim says.

A man stole from his workplace to build his own business empire, and now wants God to kill his staff who successfully siphoned millions from that business. It just doesn't work that way.

> *"You therefore who teach another, do you not teach yourself? You who preach that a man should not steal, do you steal? You who say, 'Do not commit adultery,' do you commit adultery?*
>
> *You who abhor idols, do you rob temples?" (Rom 2:21-22).*

These are pointed questions from God's word!

How I wish many Pastors knew the risk of raising some prayer points in their churches. If only they knew how close they were to picking scores of dead bodies, had God answered their judgmental prayers, they wouldn't raise them with such glee. Many who judge others deserve worse judgment themselves. Permit me to say that even some Pastors would not have been spared.

How I wish many Pastors knew the risk of raising some prayer points in their churches. If only they knew how close they were to picking scores of dead bodies.

I admonish that we return to God, clean our ways, walk in love and watch God fight our battles for us.

# 4

# THE LORD, THE LAW,
# AND THE PROPHETS

As we noted in the previous chapter, some aspects of the law and some activities of the prophets of old are indefensible in the light of our new life in Christ. When Moses and Elijah, representing the Jewish law and the prophetic tradition of the Old Testament respectively appeared in the Mount of transfiguration in the Gospel narratives, the disciples sought to place them on the same pedestal as the Lord Jesus. God had to intervene, telling Peter: the only person you are to listen to is my beloved Son. The law and the prophet, though important, are secondary to the person of the Messiah. It follows that anyone who comes to Christ today must settle the primacy of Christ in their heart. To do otherwise is to remain a child in need of tutelage.

*Wherefore the law was our school master to bring us unto Christ, that we might be justified by faith.*

*But after faith is come, we are no longer under a
school master*

*(Galatians 3:24-25,KJV).*

Ours, we must insist, is a higher calling, for the Bible states
that the law was our schoolmaster to lead us unto true
perfection in Christ. *For Christ is the end of the law for
righteousness to everyone who believes (Romans 10:4).*

The coming of Christ, therefore, marks the end of the Law.
The Lord Jesus himself is the Lord of the law. Even the law
is subject to him.

Christ came as a fulfillment of the law and the imperfections
therein were made perfect in Christ Jesus who brought us
into a brand new covenant.

In Heb.1:1, Paul reiterated that in times of old, God spoke
through His servants, the prophets, but now He has spoken
with finality through His Son.

Therefore, both the law and the prophets, having played their
roles in the old dispensation, are completely subject to
Christ.

While the law and the prophets were prototypes and shadows
which ultimately pointed us to Christ, they were not perfect
and could not give life, until Christ came.

*For the law made nothing perfect; on the other
hand, there is the bringing in of a better hope.
through which we draw near to God. (Heb. 7:19).*

In essence, it's only in Christ and Christ alone that we have a clear picture of what the law and the prophets typified and how, going forward, we can walk in newness of life.

In the Sermon on the Mount, which is evident in Matthew Chapters 5, 6 and 7, Jesus referred to the laws God gave through Moses, and then expressed what it now is, starting with him. He is the fulfilment of the law and the prophets.

*"Do not think that I came to destroy the law or the prophets. I did not come to destroy but to fulfill"*

*(Matthew 5:17).*

There is no contradiction here. The law and the prophets have spoken, acting as the school master pointing us to Christ.

The Lord Jesus having fulfilled the law and its requirements by His supreme sacrifice ushered in a new covenant. Henceforth, only Him can we hear and follow: no longer the prophets or the law.

**There is no contradiction here. The law and the prophets have spoken, acting as the school master pointing us to Christ.**

## Transfiguration Mount: The Meeting of the Three

In no other place in Scriptures did God reiterate the foregoing fact other than at the Mount of Transfiguration. At the mount was the gathering of the three; *the Lord, the law and the prophet.*

As Christ was transfigured before the three disciples; Peter, James and John, two personalities appeared with Him; Moses, representing the Law, and Elijah, representing the Prophets.

When Peter saw the three together, all in a transfigured state, he remarked,

> *'...Lord, it is good for us to be here; If you wish, let us make here three tabernacles: one for You, one for Moses, and one for Elijah'*
>
> *(Matt 17:4).*

But as he spoke, God interrupted him by speaking from heaven.

> *While he was still speaking, behold, a bright cloud overshadowed them, and suddenly a voice out of the cloud, saying 'This is My beloved Son in whom I am well pleased, HEAR HIM' (Matt 17:5, emphasis mine).*

What message was God passing across to Peter and to us here?

It is this: Neither the law as represented by Moses, nor the Prophets, as represented by Elijah, have any more say forthwith. Only Christ the Son of God can speak with finality on any issue.

This is instructive. While we will forever learn from the law and the prophets, Jesus is the final authority on all matters concerning them. To follow the law and the prophets when they are not in tandem with Christ's life and teachings is no longer tenable or acceptable. What was permissible or right in the old dispensation could be outright wrong in the new.

## Jesus and the Law

The Old Testament prophets in declaring God's counsel always said *"Thus saith the Lord..."* However, when Jesus came, he never used the phrase. Not even once. He spoke as one who had authority. *"Verily, verily I say unto you... Moses said... but I say..."*

**Prophets in the Old Testament spoke *for the Lord*, but Jesus in the New Testament spoke as the Lord.**

Prophets in the Old Testament spoke *for the Lord*, but Jesus in the New Testament spoke *as the Lord.* He spoke with such authority and audacity that people said *"... No man ever spoke like this Man"* (John 7:46).

In the Gospel of Matthew, chapter 5 alone, we heard Jesus make the following statements five times.

> *Ye have heard that it was said of the old time..., but I say unto you...It has been said..., but I say unto you...*"

In these statements, Jesus put away the old that he may establish the new.

You probably can see the direction in which I am taking this issue on the supremacy of Jesus and how it intersects with discourse on judgmental prayers. Before we turn to the prayers, let me make a final point from the Lord's sermon.

The Words of Jesus on Marble:

*"You have heard that it was said, 'You shall love your neighbor and hate your enemy.' But I say to you, love your enemies, bless those who curse you, do good to those who hate you, and pray for those who spitefully use you and persecute you. That you may be sons of your Father in heaven; for He makes His sun rise on the evil and on the good, and sends rain on the just and on the unjust. For if you love those who love you, what reward have you? Do not even the tax collectors do the same? And if you greet your brethren only, what do you do more than others? Do not even the tax collectors do so? Therefore you shall be perfect just as your Father in heaven is perfect"*

*(Matthew 5:43-48).*

This is the word of the Lord from the mouth of the Lord Himself. He left no room for the hatred of our enemies. In the new covenant, God has placed us above the baseline unto a higher calling. We would rather love our enemies, pray for them and do them a whole world of good in return for hatred, persecution and the like.

It is unthinkable how we got around these clear injunctions of the Lord to justify raining down of curses, fire and brimstone on human beings dubbed enemies. How volumes of books emerged on how to shoot them down, destroy them and their families?

I have a guess: *We have taken some of the prayers and lifestyles of the prophets of old and adopted them.* But many of them just cannot apply in the new dispensation. Permit me to say they are not totally right. The Captain of our Salvation has spoken differently. It is he we will hear.

Perhaps, one of the best interpreters of this perspective of the Lord Jesus, Apostle Paul wrote:

> *Therefore 'If your enemy is hungry, feed him; If he is thirsty, give him a drink. For in so doing you will heap coals of fire on his head'. Do not be overcome by evil, but overcome evil with good (Romans 12:20-21).*

In the closing sections of this book, we will deal extensively with how to handle enemies in the light of scriptures. But permit me to say at this point: *When you confront evil with evil, you have come to meet your enemy in his terrain where evil reigns. You may succeed in harming him, but you could get harmed too in their territory. However, when you confront evil with good, you operate at a level that makes you untouchable to the enemy under any circumstance.*

When the coals of the fire of judgment hit your enemy from head to toe, nothing shall by any means hurt you.

## Jesus and the Prophets

In the book of Luke chapter 9, we have the interesting account of some disciples of the Lord who sought His permission to call down fire from heaven on an entire village and they quoted a prophetic act from the Old Testament to back up their proposal.

What was the villagers' offence? They denied Jesus the right of passage through their territory. While the Lord took it calmly and simply turned back to go by another village, the two sons of Zebedee (rightly called the "sons of thunder") would have none of that. These villagers must be severely dealt with, in their thinking. Please note that this was in defense of their Lord. So they popped the big question:

*Now it came to pass, when the time had come for Him to be received up, that He steadfastly set His face to go to Jerusalem, and sent messengers before His face. And as they went, they entered a village of the Samaritans, to prepare for Him. But they did not receive Him, because His face was set for the journey to Jerusalem. And when His disciples James and John saw this, they said,* **"Lord, do You want us to command fire to come down from heaven and consume them, just as Elijah did?" But He turned and rebuked them, and said, "You do not know what manner of spirit you are of. For the Son of Man did not come to**

*destroy men's lives but to save them."* And they
*went to another village*

*(Luke 9:51-56, emphasis mine).*

## Jesus Turned

Think of this. *Jesus turned!* To turn means he had already
faced his way and was already ahead of the disciples,
resolved to go by another route while the disciples foot-
dragged, thinking through what punishment is best to mete
out to this people.

Jesus turned! He turned swiftly when he heard what he never
imagined a follower of his could conceive: destroying an
entire village just for mere denial of entry or passage.

Jesus turned! This matter cannot wait for another time, he
seemed to have thought to himself. There is no better time to
confront this crucial issue than now. It required a quick and
sharp response once and for all.

This may be why this book is confronting this subject right
now, headlong. Could it be that God has been turning away
from our fire-spitting judgmental prayers against people for
whom he died? Is God not shocked by the content of our
many prayers? What would he do to these many volumes
already written on how to destroy our enemies, as if we lived
in the old dispensation?

Jesus rebuked James and John sharply to the hearing of us
all. God has renewed us and made us of a different spiritual
stock that makes the destruction of people a foreign entity.

If destruction in the name of God by the prophets struck God's fear into the hearts of men, that was then. In this new order, such prayer frameworks are outdated. We are of a different spirit. It's no longer an eye for an eye, but overcoming evil with good.

> **If destruction in the name of God by the prophets struck God's fear into the hearts of men, that was then.**

We can confidently say, therefore, that these vindictive judgmental prayers people pray because the prophets prayed them are doubtlessly wrong. I doubt the Holy Spirit inspired these many volumes written on how to rain fire and curses on human enemies. It is simply not the spirit we are made of.

We may need to ask ourselves these pertinent questions; Did Christ pray judgmental prayers? Did the Apostles of Christ pray them? In the Book of Acts, when the apostles were imprisoned and threatened never to preach anymore in the name of Christ, did they rain down fire and curses on the Sanhendrin and ask God to kill them all? No. Rather they prayed for power to disseminate the message of Christ and his resurrection with greater boldness (See Acts 4:24-31).

## Elijah and The Massacre

We need to re-visit the Elijah story to fully understand why Christ dissociated himself from some of the seeming excesses of the prophets.

In second Kings Chapter one, Elijah called down fire from heaven twice and killed a total of one hundred and two soldiers. This was the incident James and John referred to. Their offence? They had the guts to deliver a verbal message from their Commander-in- Chief to the man of God without molesting him in whatever way. The message to Elijah was simple:

> *Then the king sent unto him a captain of fifty with his fifty men. So he went up to him; and there he was, sitting on the top of a hill. And he spoke to him: "Man of God, the king has said, 'Come down.'"*
>
> *So Elijah answered and said to the Captain of fifty, "If I am a man of God, then let fire come down from heaven and consume you and your fifty men." And fire came down from heaven and consumed him and his fifty.*
>
> *(2 Kings 1:9-10).*

Another set of fifty was sent with the same message and they met with the same fate, their captain not excluded (See 2 Kings 1:11-12).

Was there anything provocative in this message? What exactly annoyed the prophet? Had the king no audacity to send for him? Is this to prove he's a man of God? Why this carnage?

When the third captain came with his fifty men, and saw dead bodies littering the whole place, he applied wisdom and pleaded with the man of God to spare their lives. He then delivered the exact message. An angel of the Lord then appeared to Elijah and instructed him to follow them and he did.

> *And the angel of the Lord said to Elijah, "Go down with him;* ***do not be not afraid of him****;" So he arose and went down with him to the king (2 Kings 1:15, emphasis mine).*

**Was there anything provocative in this message? What exactly annoyed the prophet? Had the king no audacity to send for him? Is this to prove he's a man of God? Why this carnage?**

So, your guess is as good as mine. Elijah brutally killed 102 innocent soldiers because he feared for his life. He thought the king would kill him and he could not trust God to protect him, so he wasted so many lives. Elijah had earlier sent a bitter message from God through the king's messengers to the king, for which, I guess the king wanted to hear directly from him. He wasn't exactly sure what the king would do to him. In fear, he unleashed mayhem, not on the king, but on the messengers. If he could call fire down at will, why not reserve it for the one who sent them—rain fire on the king at the palace if he tried any game.

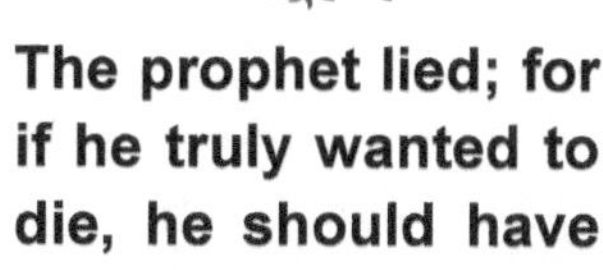

**The prophet lied; for if he truly wanted to die, he should have waited for Jezebel and not run for his dear life.**

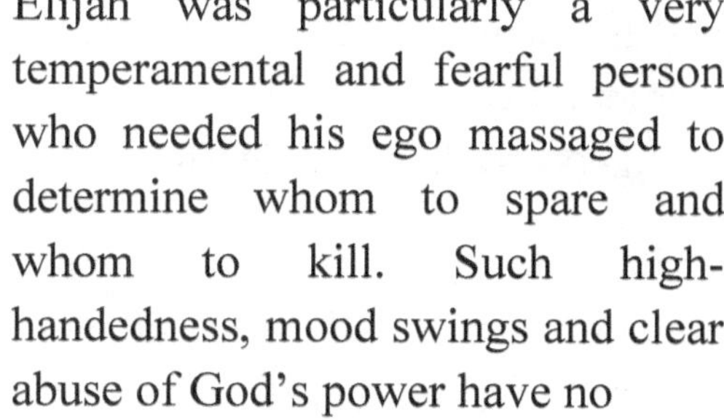

Elijah was particularly a very temperamental and fearful person who needed his ego massaged to determine whom to spare and whom to kill. Such high-handedness, mood swings and clear abuse of God's power have no

place in Christ. A man who had just killed 450 prophets of Baal took to his heels when a woman, Jezebel, threatened to kill him. He became so disgruntled, complained bitterly against God and even wished to die. *"... And he prayed that he might die, and said, 'It is enough! Now LORD, take my life, for I am no better than my fathers'"* (1 Kings 19:4).

The prophet lied; for if he truly wanted to die, he should have waited for Jezebel and not run for his dear life. That's an OT prophet for you and this is definitely not the kind of spirit we are made of. We walk in the Spirit and live by kingdom principles, not ruled by feelings and emotions. And the fruit of the Spirit is love, joy, peace, gentleness, patience, kindness. Not callousness and chaos. Never!

Have you stopped to consider the number of women who suddenly became widows and the numerous children rendered fatherless because of the unbridled use of power by the man of God?

Perhaps you can imagine the wailing in many homes and the mourning in communities over men who never went to war? Can you see why Jesus distanced himself from this prophet and his actions? Elijah shed the blood of war in peace. The soldiers just got killed for nothing, the same way those villagers would have died for nothing.

Elijah's action is in no wise different from the activities of suicide bombers of our days, who turn explosives on innocent people whose sole crime was being in the right place at the wrong time.

> **Perhaps you can imagine the wailing in many homes and the mourning in communities over men who never went to war? Can you see why Jesus distanced himself from this prophet and his actions?**

Jesus cannot but distance Himself from these, and his disciples should not emulate these actions of the prophet. No! Not in a covenant that ushered in God's love through Christ's death. He has said it all. *Ye know not what manner of spirit ye are made of? For the Son of Man is not come to destroy men's lives but to save them.* Period!

## Elisha and The Great Slaughter

On that day in Bethel, it played out like a horror movie.

*And he (Elisha) went up from there unto Bethel and as he was going up by the way, there came forth little children out of the city, and mocked him and said 'Go up, thou bald head; go up, thou bald head. And he turned back, and looked to them, and cursed them in the name of the Lord. And there came forth two she-bears out of the wood and tare forty and two children of them. And he went from thence to Mount Carmel, and from hence, returned to Samaria"*

*(2 Kings 2; 23-25 KJV).*

Here we go again. These "no-nonsense" prophets seemed to have so much going for them and they got away with it.

It played out like a horror movie. Elisha, freshly anointed with a double portion was passing through Bethel. A group of little children gathered to jeer at him saying, "Go up, bald head", in apparent reference to Elijah who has just been carried up to heaven by chariots of fire. To be clear, these children were wrong, very wrong, not honouring an elderly person, much more, a man of God.

Just like Jesus, Elisha turned. Rather than rebuke them as a father, he, in anger, pronounced a deadly curse on them.

Instantly, two ferocious bears came out of the woods and tore 42 children. Forty-two badly torn bodies of children littered the street with blood splattered everywhere. It looked more like a war zone, more like a genocide. It was a blood bath unprecedented, but Elisha simply walked away, continuing in his journey, leaving parents to mourn and bury their children.

Can you imagine that your desires are patterned after Elisha?

The prophets of old were made of stuff unknown in Christ's love ecology. They consistently exhibited the spirit of vengeance and holy anger in the name of the Lord. While they did so much good, they sometimes left much devastation and carnage on their trail. They took no prisoners. Undoubtedly, the actions of these children were unjustified, but ending their lives so violently was uncalled for.

**Did I hear you say, "It served those children right"? You may not be wrong, but had every child guilty of mockery died, fewer people would be holding this book now.**

The man of God unleashed great pain, agony, wailing and devastation on a very historic city. Many were rendered childless. The nightmares will not disappear quickly and they will forever remember that one man of God passed through the land and caused them much pain. His name was Elisha.

Did I hear you say, "It served those children right"? You may not be wrong, but had every child guilty of mockery died, fewer people would be holding this book now. Don't you think so?

And so in Bethel, "flags" were flown at half-mast. Men and women wept uncontrollably, tearing their garments and wearing sack cloth and ashes, not for their sins or a natural disaster, but because of a man of God who passed by and left a trail of blood and tears…

Let us simply put Jesus the Lord in Elisha's shoes. Would the Lord have cursed a group of jeering children? We all know the answer. It's an emphatic no. He would only have rebuked them.

With Him, mercy prevails over judgment.

He said "I will have mercy and not sacrifice" (Matthew 9:13).

And he wants us to walk in His steps.

> *For to this you were called, because Christ also suffered for us, leaving us an example, that you should follow His steps:*
> *"Who committed no sin,*
> *Nor was deceit found in His mouth";*
> *who, **when He was reviled, did not revile in return; when He suffered, He did not threaten,** but committed Himself to Him who judges righteously (1 Peter 2:21-23 emphasis mine).*

Let us leave judgment to Him that judges righteously. Let mercy prevail over judgment in our lives. Let's be quick to show mercy. We must be sympathetic and have compassion on people whose faith are weaker compared to ours, so we can in love lead them to higher realms of faith in God. That is the spirit we are made of.

## Elisha and The Unbelieving Man

**What was Elisha's reaction? He instantly handed the man a death sentence,**

It was Elisha again in Samaria. In 2 Kings Chapter 7, a man could not muster the faith to believe God when Elisha prophesied the miracle of abundance within 24 hours, to a nation reeling in deep economic upheaval and hunger. He could not have been the only unbeliever in Samaria. More than half the people might not have believed. The man's mistake was voicing his unbelief. *"Look, if the Lord would make windows in heaven, could this thing be?" he asked (2 Kings 7:2a).*

What was Elisha's reaction? He instantly handed the man a death sentence, ***"In fact, you shall see it with your eyes, but you shall not eat of it"*** *(2 Kings 7:2b, emphasis mine).*

He could have easily said, *Wait and see.*

> *Now the king had appointed the officer on whose hand he leaned to have charge of the gate. But the people trampled him in the gate, and he died, just as the man of God had said, who spoke when the king came down to him*
>
> *(2 Kings 7:17).*

Elisha was ruthless. He could not allow fools any breathing space. But we know the new life in Christ gives no room for such deadly a temperament.

Our Lord Jesus who lives in us by His Spirit, whose example we follow would say no such thing. So why would we? When Thomas, one of the disciples who walked with him on earth expressed strong doubts about his resurrection, He did not come down raining curses on him or disqualify him from ministry altogether. He was not even angry. He reached out to him and the doubting Thomas became a great hero of faith. He said to him, *Thomas, here am I, alive and well. See me, touch me if you wish.* He came that the unbelieving may believe, not that the unbelieving may die.

Rather than condemn Thomas for doubting the foundation of the Christian faith, the Lord lovingly showed him the evidence of a resurrected life. Jesus's response to Thomas did not only convince the disciple, it also made Thomas the major agent of the spread of the Gospel in Southern India.

The approach of Jesus was love and love never fails.

Little wonder the *sons of thunder,* James and John were transformed to become great pillars of the faith in the early church. Jesus' life and love transformed them eventually.

John, who later came to be known as the *Apostle of love,* wrote 5 books of the New Testament and love is the central theme. He was the disciple whom Jesus loved and that love he gladly shared with all.

> **He came that the unbelieving may believe, not that the unbelieving may die.**

James was the administrative head of the early church. He exhibited great leadership skills, fruit and gifts of the Spirit.

He laid down his life as a martyr, not threatening those who killed him for his faith in Jesus.

May God's investment in us also yield great returns of righteousness and love.

**Wow! This is the original undiluted *"operation-no-mercy-somersault-and-die- by-fire-by force"* prayer against an enemy**

## Now Spot the Difference!

On a final note, please find below a prayer said by another prophet, Jeremiah, against his "enemies" who persecuted him:

> *Therefore deliver up their children to the famine, and pour out their blood by the force of the sword; and let their wives be bereaved of children, and be widows; and let their men be put to death; let their young men be slain by the sword in battle... Lord, thou knowest all their counsel against me to slay me: forgive not their iniquity, neither blot out their sins from your sight but let them be overthrown before thee; deal with them in the time of your anger (Jer. 18:21-23 KJV).*

Wow! This is the original undiluted *"operation-no-mercy-somersault-and-die-by-fire-by force"* prayer against an enemy.

These are strong words. The prophet wanted total destruction not only of his enemies, but also of their families, their children, their lineage. God must never forgive their sins too so that they can rot forever in hell, all because they *counselled against him.*

**We cannot totally blame the prophets. They served God, and were zealous for Him and could not tolerate evil.**

I can imagine that you are as surprised as I am as you read those damaging prayers by the renowned prophet. Now can you spot the difference between this prayer and the prayer of Stephen for his own enemies when his life was being violently cut short?

I am talking of Stephen's one-liner: *Lord, hold not this sin to their charge.*

The difference is crystal clear. It's the difference between life and death, between the old and the new covenants. One called for vengeance and death, the other, forgiveness, love and life. This too is the life we have been called to.

We cannot totally blame the prophets. They served God, and were zealous for Him and could not tolerate evil. They did it all in defense of God's name but they operated under a faulty and moribund covenant that bore little light comparative to ours.

We ought to thank God that we have not just found light in Christ. We are the light of the world. Our prayer altars must henceforth reflect this light.

If you have come this far with me, I am certain you now lack the capacity to pray such prayers as Prophet Jeremiah did. We have known the truth and it has set us free.

Henceforth, let us walk as children of light.

> *That you may become blameless and harmless, children of God without fault in the midst of a crooked and perverse generation, among whom you shine as lights in the world (Philippians 2:15).*

Amen!

# AHEAD OF THEIR GENERATION:
# DAVID

Not everyone in the Old Testament was cantankerous like Elijah or impulsive like Elisha. There are many whose lives and activities were written for our examples. These men and women lived in the old dispensation, yet they possessed the heart of a New Testament saint. They lived under the law, yet were grace-compliant. The requirement of the law says "an eye for an eye", but while under that law, they received the power to be gracious, to love, and to forgive. They were ahead of their generation. They had entered a New Testament experience while in the old. They tasted the power of the world to come.

**They lived under the law, yet were grace-compliant.**

Paul, in the book of Hebrews, spoke about men who had already tasted the power of the world to come while still in the flesh (6:5). In the same vein, we have some Old Testament saints who experienced the life that was to come in Christ Jesus. These notable saints pose a great challenge to us who have received God's enabling grace to walk in righteousness and true holiness.

As we do a brief study of men as it affects the focus of this book, the question to answer should be: If the Old Testament that was done away with, due to its imperfection, could produce such glorious lives, how much more should the New Testament saint exceed in glory. Paul wrote:

> *If the ministry of condemnation had glory, the ministry of righteousness exceed much more in glory. For even what was made glorious had no glory in this respect, because of the glory that excels.*
>
> *For if what is passing away was glorious, what remains is much more glorious*
>
> *(2 Cor. 3:9-11).*

Yes, we had Old Testament saints that were New Testament compliant. They exhibited Christ-likeness, the type we all in this generation should emulate. These men towered high in the light of the issues under discourse: the issues of judgmental prayers, love for enemies, forgiveness and praying aright. They all, no doubt, had their shortcomings, but the virtues that gave them a good report through faith is worthy of perusal.

## DAVID

Ahead of the pack was David, a man after God's own heart, a man who pursued life in the Spirit, despite being king.

**He understood spirituality, which is making God the centre of one's life, conduct and achievements.**

He was a God-chaser. He pursued after God all his life and gave Him a pride of place in his heart. No wonder he was ahead of his generation.

He understood spirituality, which is making God the centre of one's life, conduct and achievements. Through him, prophecies concerning the coming of the Lord and His Kingdom were brought forth, and the Lord was proud to call Himself the root of David (see Rev 22:16).

### David's Thirst for God

David's passion for God was unequalled. His words speak for him.

*As the hart pants for the water brooks, so pants my soul for You, O God. My soul thirsts for God, for the living God. When shall I come and appear before God? My tears have been my food day and night, while they continually say to me "where is your God?" (Psalm 42:1).*

May this kind of hunger for God and God alone be deeply manifest in our generation. We seem to lack this kind of hunger in our days. We thirst and hunger only after riches, fame, worldly possessions. We crave the blessings of God, not the God of the blessings. An average believer today wants to use God to achieve his own goals, not God using the believer to achieve God's own goals. God, for many today, is a means to an end. I once heard a preacher say *God is a game*. David obviously understood and knew God in a special way, read what he says:

> *One thing I have desired of the LORD, that will I seek: That I may dwell in the house of the LORD all the days of my life, to behold the beauty of the LORD and to inquire in His temple"* (Psalm 27:4).

It is God hundred percent, nothing else. Every other issue of life stems from there. May we possess this kind of heart today.

What are the proofs of his experience of the world to come? Hear these words:

**"Create in me a new heart O God, and renew a right spirit within me...** (Psalm 51:10). To have a new heart is to experience the new birth, a New Testament experience.

**"Cast me not away from your presence, Oh Lord...** (Psalm 51:11). He dwelt in God's presence, cherished it, and cried out to God when he seemed to have lost it. He simply could not imagine a life outside of His presence. Even in the new covenant, do we cherish His presence this much?

**Take not your Holy Spirit from me...** (Psalm 51:11). This is getting serious. David knew the Holy Spirit, had the Holy Spirit, valued the preciousness of the Holy Spirit in his heart, and can't imagine a life devoid of Him. As New Testament saints, is this even our cry?

**Restore unto me the joy of your salvation...–** (Psalm 51:12). This sums it all. *David was saved.* You don't ask to be restored what was never there. As in the new birth, he experienced God's salvation and its joy, and when he sinned and lost it, he cried to God for its restoration. While some New Testament believers live in sin, justify it and feel no sense of remorse or godly sorrow, here is an Old Testament saint who would not regard iniquity in his heart, but cried for mercy.

> **This sums it all. *David was saved***

**Then will I teach transgressors your way, and sinners shall be converted unto thee...** (Psalm 51:13).

Even in the old, David partook of the great commission. He preached to sinners to be converted unto God.

**Open thou my eyes, that I may behold wondrous things out of your law** (Psalm 119:18). This is revelation knowledge. As an old saint, he had deep insights into God's word which inspired him also to be moved by the Holy Ghost to write God's word to us. There were numerous prophecies written by David concerning Christ. A man operating under a doomed covenant had experienced the power of the world to come.

If, as I have tried to show, David truly experienced the life to come, let's see how this life manifested in his words and conduct with those around him.

## Saul: When the Hunter Became the Hunted

It's a familiar story. David killed Goliath and became an instant celebrity in Israel; his name became a household name, even among Israel's enemies. The Philistines won't forget him in a hurry. He was loved, he was feared and his name was on the lips of everyone. Saul the king envied him, saw him as a major threat to his throne, and then began a massive manhunt for David's life that lasted over a decade. At some point, David had to leave Israel's territory altogether and sought refuge in the land of the Philistines, whose Goliath he had earlier killed. By a stroke of divine favour, they did him no harm. His ways pleased the Lord and his enemies were at peace with him.

Saul hunted David from pillar to post. He was vengeful. Every friend or helper of David became Saul's enemy. So blinded was Saul by jealousy that he became estranged from his son Jonathan and daughter Micah. He ordered the killing of 70 priests that wore the ephod, all because of a soul that did him no wrong. David was greatly distressed, he ran for his life, but God was with him and he blessed him with a band of men who were fiercely loyal and were ready to die for him.

A day however came when God did a turnaround, for a purpose. God reversed the roles and David the hunted became the hunter. While pursuing after David, Saul found himself within David's territory, unbeknownst. Being weary from his hunt, he reclined in a cave with his entire army. In no time, they were fast asleep. In fact, the word of God called it a *deep sleep from the Lord* (1 Sam 26:12). Now it was David's rare chance to kill his enemy, put an end to this endless chase and fast track his way to the throne God had anointed him for. To the utter shock of David's men, he refused to take vengeance on Saul, to kill him. This would have been justified under the law which reads "an eye for an eye".

> *Then the men of David said to him, "This is the day of which the Lord said to you, 'Behold, I will deliver your enemy into your hand, that you may do to him as it seems good to you.'" And David arose and secretly cut off a corner of Saul's robe.*

> *Now it happened afterward that David's heart troubled him because he had cut Saul's robe. And he said to his men, 'The Lord forbid that I should do this thing to my master, the LORD's anointed, to stretch out my hand against him, seeing he is the anointed of the Lord.' So David restrained his servants with these words, and did not allow them to rise against Saul... (1 Sam. 24:4-7).*

David's men did not understand this principle we are discussing now. To them, it was their master's turn to avenge himself.

David stoutly refused to avenge himself by killing Saul. Ending Saul's life would have brought instant end to his sufferings and catapult him towards the throne. But David would rather prolong his sufferings by many more years than be guilty of the blood of God's anointed. When David made bold to confront Saul, hear what he said to him: ...*Moreover, my father, see! Yes, see the corner of your robe in my hand! For in that I cut off the corner of your robe, and did not kill you, know and see that there is neither evil nor rebellion in my hand, and I have not sinned against you. Yet you hunt my life to take it.* **Let the LORD judge between you and me, and let the LORD avenge me on you. But my hand shall not be against you** *(1 Samuel 24:11- 12, emphasis mine).*

See how David left vengeance to God, and this has been our main emphasis in this book. That leaving vengeance to God is His expectation of the New Testament saint. This is the model Jesus the Lord portrayed in His teachings, and here, David in the Old Testament was an embodiment of it.

*That was not all.*

Not long after, David again underwent the same test in 1 Sam 26. Saul's life was again delivered unto him, but he refused to kill him. It was as if God repeated the test to be sure David truly got it right. He did. He again passed God's test. He stood his ground, refusing to avenge himself. Even Saul could not believe David's magnanimity, he admitted;

> *"...You are more righteous than I; for you have rewarded me with good, whereas I have rewarded you with evil. And you have shown this day how you have dealt well with me;* ***for when the LORD delivered me into your hand, you did not kill me.***

*For if a man finds his enemy, will he let him get away safely? Therefore may the LORD reward you with good for what you have done to me this day"* (1 Sam 24:17-19 emphasis mine).

Saul admitted David rewarded him good for evil, not once, but on two occasions. Paul, in the book of Romans admonished: *be not overcome of evil, but overcome evil with good.* Was this not what David did? This is God's expectation for the New Testament saint as exhibited by David. We can't do less.

That was not all.

## A Song for Saul

When David was informed of the death of Saul and his children in a battle with the Philistines, he could not celebrate. He rent his clothes and deeply mourned the man who made life so unbearable for him. His watchword was never to avenge himself but to allow God to be the judge. And even when God judged, he was not trying to stifle his joy, he truly mourned. That is the New Testament spirit laid down for us to follow. Did the Bible not say:

*Do not rejoice when your enemy falls, and do not let your heart be glad when he stumbles; Lest the Lord see it, and it displease Him, and he turn away his wrath from him*

*(Prov. 24:17-18).*

I am sure that is in your Bible as well. That God said he must not catch you and me rejoicing over the fall of an enemy? Why then do we hear people share with relish testimonies of the demise and fall of their enemies and the people of God clap in rejoicing?

Obviously, David's respect for God's person and for the office of God's anointed made a lot of difference in this case. Rather than kill Saul in retaliation, he composed a poem, a dirge, for Saul and his son, Jonathan. In it he extolled Saul's virtues, making no reference whatsoever to the years of his vindictiveness towards him. He possibly understood that his battle was not against flesh and blood. What a man! He even called Saul mighty.

> *"Ye daughters of Israel, weep over Saul, who clothed you in scarlet, with luxury, who put ornaments of gold upon your apparel… how the mighty have fallen, and the weapons of war perished (2 Sam 1:24,27).*

These are strong character traits exhibited by a thirty-year-old man that are worthy of emulation in Christendom today.

This was not all

**Rather than kill Saul in retaliation, he composed a poem, a dirge, for Saul and his son, Jonathan.**

## Blessing an Arch-enemy

David reigned as king over Israel for 40 years. Many years into his reign, this man with a heart of gold was so free of bitterness that he yet cried:

*"... Is there still any who is left of the house of Saul, that I may show him kindness for Jonathan's sake?*

*(2 Sam 9:1).*

What a challenge to our generation! This is *Agape Love* at its peak, the love that never fails. At the height of David's glory on the throne, when even the best of men are intoxicated with power and forget their friends, David sought yet again to bless the house of his arch- enemy posthumously, even when they were not alive to see what has become of their legacies.

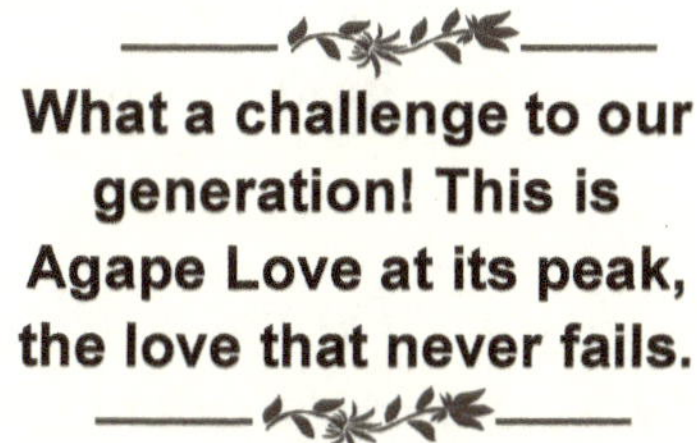

**What a challenge to our generation! This is Agape Love at its peak, the love that never fails.**

To honour Jonathan's memory, David was ready to bless anyone, just anyone still living, from the house of Saul. This is the height of Christian love. No bitterness, no fight-to-finish, and no vengeance. If a man under the old covenant could do this, how about us? There is no room for judgmental prayers, death of enemies, joy over enemies' misfortunes, wicked testimonies, and misguided prayers. Vengeance belongs only to God.

Still this wasn't all.

## Mephibosheth: Palace Resident

By providence, a man named *Mephibosheth*, a son of Jonathan was found to be alive. He became lame on both feet when the nurse who tried to escape with him in order to save his life fell. As a lad, his two feet became lame and he possibly crawled on his hands (See 2 Sam 4:4).

On hearing Mephibosheth was handicapped and living in faraway Lodebar, David could just have rehabilitated him by providing some care for him for the rest of his life. That would have been supreme magnanimity to the seed of an enemy. He could also have ordered Ziba (the Chief servant of Saul) to restore all that belonged to his father and grandfather to him. This also would have been honourable.

Not David.

This Old Testament saint rose above the flesh and selfish desires, above all human sentiments to show kindness to the handicapped.

> *So David said to him (Mephibosheth), "Do not fear for I will surely show you kindness for Jonathan, your fathers sake and will restore you all the land of Saul your grandfather; AND YOU SHALL EAT BREAD AT MY TABLE CONTINUALLY"*
>
> *(2 Sam 9:7 emphasis mine).*

This is the testimony of the man after God's own heart. Little wonder he was that called by God. This is the man who extended the love and goodness of God to the seed of his arch-enemy. Mephibosheth thus became a *Permanent Resident* in the palace. His wobbled legs were no eye-sore to David.

Dragging himself to sit at dinner table was a delight to this king of all times. Little wonder Jesus the Lord would gladly refer to Himself as both the Son of David and the Root of David (See Rev. 22:16).

**Mephibosheth thus became a *Permanent Resident* in the palace. His wobbled legs were no eye-sore to David. Dragging himself to sit at dinner table was a delight to this king of all times.**

What a challenge to our generation! It is a great challenge to me and I hope you see it that way too. In this issue of love and forgiveness, let us all who have the love of God shed abroad in our hearts by the Holy Spirit rise to demonstrate it to a godless, loveless world.

If an Old Testament saint lived the new covenant life, God forbids that we, being New Testament saints, should live by old standards. *"By this shall all men know that ye are my disciples when ye have love one for another."*

Christ's Love must trump the Law.

# AHEAD OF THEIR GENERATION:
# ABRAHAM

The Patriarch, Abraham, was another notable example of saints who were ahead of their generation. Abraham was not only the father of faith; he was also a man who demonstrated the kind of love and forgiveness that is the focus of this book. The love of God, shed abroad in his heart in his relationship with Lot stands out as a testimony to our generation.

## Abraham and Lot's Growing Family

Lot was Abraham's nephew, the son of his deceased's brother, Haram. In Genesis chapter 12, when God called Abraham out of his kindred and father's house, he took Lot and his household with him. There were several remarkable issues in their relationship from which we could learn. First, even though Sarah, Abraham's wife, was barren meaning Abraham was childless; Lot had a wife and was blessed with children. Lot's fruitful family status, comparably, did not constitute any threat to Abraham's family in whatever way. They dwelt together peacefully, showing maturity in handling any tension such situation could bring. The Bible did not record any squabbles in their relationship. The only record of strife was between their herdsmen and not with the two.

Such is rare in our days. And it ought to be an indictment on our profession of faith in Christ.

A relationship like this would have bred much envy, jealousy, bickering and in-fighting that would have led to a parting much earlier than they did. Abraham and Sarah's maturity in the face of Lot's growing family is laudable. They were rest assured in the promises of God to them and this eliminated pettiness, envy or jealousy. If we all are rest assured in God's word that reads: "I will not leave you nor forsake you" and "I know the plans I have for you", may be, just may be this schism in the body will stop. But greed and covetousness has blinded many.

Even when God has blessed men with good things of life, enough can never be enough for them. Wrong association keeps many in an endless chase for filthy lucre, competing with the world and with one another. We have Abraham as our father and he is worthy of emulation.

## Lot's Growing Fortune

Under Abraham, Lot was given a free rein to grow to his highest potential in business and merchandise. Leveraging on his closeness to a man in covenant relationship with God,

Lot grew just as Abraham grew. Abraham never felt threatened to stay in his way, or stifle his growth. He allowed him free rein, not mindful of the latter's increasing prosperity.

> *Lot also, who went with Abram, had flocks and herds and tents. Now the land was not able to support them that they might dwell together, for their possessions were so great, that they could not dwell together. And there was strife between the herdsmen of Abram's livestock and the herdsmen of Lot's livestock. The Canaanites and the Perrizites then dwelt in the land (Gen 13:5-7).*

These are unlikely developments in our days. How many will allow a nephew, son of a late brother such unfettered growth under him without trying to restrain him? Abraham must have refused to listen to many strife-peddlers who must have cautioned him against Lot. He'll be told his true motives are to take over Abraham's dynasty and inherit it since Abraham had no child of his. Not Abraham.

**How many will allow a nephew, son of a late brother such unfettered growth under him without trying to restrain him?**

He has lifted his eyes unto the Most High God, the possessor of all heaven and earth; he will not be deterred from God's ways. Not until they had to separate on account of largeness, they co- habited peacefully. The credit goes to Abraham.

## Abraham's Legendary Humility

**Lot therefore squandered the only opportunity he had to repay a man under whose love and tutelage he had become great.**

Now this: When separation became inevitable on account of unending quarrels among their herdsmen, it was Abraham who made a peace move, giving Lot his much younger nephew the privilege of making the first choice of where to migrate. One would have thought that Lot should have insisted that his Uncle and benefactor of many decades make the first choice. After all, Abraham took him up when he lost his father and nurtured him to greatness. With age still on Lot's side, should he not have allowed Abraham to make the first choice, helping him to go where life would be less stressful for this great benefactor at old age?

Shockingly, he did not.

Lot therefore squandered the only opportunity he had to repay a man under whose love and tutelage he had become great. He gladly accepted Abraham's offer and consequently made a tragic choice in the flesh, for which he lived to forever regret.

Indeed, to be carnally minded is death.

*And Lot lifted his eyes and saw all the plain of Jordan, that it was well watered everywhere, (before the LORD destroyed Sodom and Gomorrah), like the garden of the LORD, like the land of Egypt as you go towards Zoar*

*(Gen 13:10).*

Lot made a very bad business decision; he chose a location that was marked out for ultimate destruction. He moved to Sodom and Gomorrah, to a people under God's judgment. And he ultimately shared their fate. With no more cover of the Abrahamic covenant, Lot became an easy prey. There is much to learn here.

**With no more cover of the Abrahamic covenant, Lot became an easy prey. There is much to learn here.**

Was Abraham bitter about Lot's choice of the most watered plains or his lack of regard and respect for his more elderly uncle? No. He respected Lot's choice and went the other way, knowing fully well that regardless of where he went, the covenant of God stands sure for him and that's what makes the difference. It was a practical demonstration of absolute trust in God and His promises. God was so moved by Abraham's actions that, no sooner Lot left, God spoke to renew His covenant with him.

*And the Lord said unto Abram, **after that Lot has separated from him,** "Lift your eyes now and look from the place where you are- northward, southward, eastward and westward; for all the land which you see, I give to you and your descendants as the dust of the earth; so that if a man could number* *the dust of the earth, then your descendants also could be numbered. Arise; walk through its length and its width, for I will give it to you (Gen 13:14-17, emphasis mine).*

## Lot's Rescue

After Lot's family and all his goods have settled in Sodom, there was a battle for the land. The kings of Sodom and Gomorrah, in league with other nations, fought against a coalition of kings. Sodom and Gomorrah were totally overrun by these rampaging kings. All the people were captured and all their goods taken as spoil. Needless to say, Lot, his entire family and all his great possessions for which he chose Sodom were all taken away (See Gen. 14).

This was Abraham's test of love and forgiveness, putting him ahead of his generation: When news got to him of Lot's capture, he could have said, *"serves him right, greedy glutton"*. Abraham did no such thing. There was no room for bitterness, vengeance in his heart. This Old Testament saint swung into action. Deploying his private army of three hundred and eighteen militias, Abraham personally led a military campaign that ousted the earlier victors and brought about the liberation of the entire people of Sodom and Gomorrah, their kings, and all their possession, *at no cost to them.* Rather than gloat over Lot's wrong choices, Abraham helped recover all that was lost.

This is how it should be in the body of Christ today, but we have allowed ourselves to be consumed by hatred and vengeance, making us unperturbed at the loss suffered by a perceived enemy within or outside the body of Christ. We want our enemies punished, they are not to go scot free, and they must suffer. This is how some of our spiritual elders taught us.

> **Abraham said 'no' to increasing his wealth by his victory. God, again, was touched by this selfless, God-centered action of Abraham that Melchizedek, a type of Christ welcomed him from the slaughter of the kings and blessed him. Could it be that when we overcome evil with our good, God always shows up to bless us?**

They taught us *operation no mercy,* not against the devil and his cohorts, but against fellow human beings who must die for offending us. And when it seems our prayers are being answered, we gloat over their misfortunes, and gleefully share testimonies of their fall. Some supposed enemies are fellow saints. My brethren, this should not be so. Christ did not come to destroy men's lives but to save them. Let's leave wickedness to the wicked and allow our light to shine above darkness.

Abraham pursued, overtook and recovered ALL for someone he could readily tag an enemy. He bluntly refused to be rewarded for his action. Is a labourer not worthy of his reward? Yet Abraham said 'no' to increasing his wealth by his victory. God, again, was touched by this selfless, God-centered action of Abraham that Melchizedek, a type of Christ welcomed him from the slaughter of the kings and blessed him. Could it be that when we overcome evil with our good, God always shows up to bless us?

*So Abraham brought back all the goods, and also brought back his brother Lot and his goods, as well as the women and the people*

*(Gen 14:16).*

Still, that was not all

## Abraham's intercession for Lot

When God determined to destroy Sodom and Gomorrah by fire because of their iniquity, the angels of destruction stopped over at Abraham's place, and hinted him of God's determinate counsel. Yet again, for the sake of Lot, Abraham stood in intercession before the Lord that God may spare the land. And when he could not secure the total deliverance of all, he pleaded with the angels not to destroy the righteous with the wicked in a bid to get Lot and his family spared. What a man! This is Christ-like love exhibited by Abraham, even before God gave the law to Moses. God's expectation is no less of us who have a better covenant established on better promises.

**Lot suffered the consequences of his wrong choices and obvious compromises in his adopted place of abode. In the end, he lost everything that had attracted him to Sodom.**

Lot suffered the consequences of his wrong choices and obvious compromises in his adopted place of abode. In the end, he lost everything that had attracted him to Sodom.

All his goods perished when God rained fire on Sodom and Gomorrah, but please note that it was not Abraham who prayed against him and wished him evil. Rather, he asked God's mercy for him and Lot was saved even though as passing through fire (See 1 Cor 3:15).

When everything went up in flames, Lot's wife could not take it. She looked back despite God's warning to the contrary and perished. Lot's two daughters who had learnt the way of the people of Sodom intoxicated their father with the intent of raising children through him. It worked. From the bastards that resulted from this unholy union came the generation of Moab and Ammon, two great nations which became sworn enemies of Israel, the descendants of Abraham. What an irony!

**Men who partook of the world to come through their faith and righteousness; Joseph, Job, Ruth, Daniel, Moses and a host of others. These manifested the new life in the old.**

Time will fail me to talk of other notable men and women who were clearly ahead of their generation. Men who partook of the world to come through their faith and righteousness; Joseph, Job, Ruth, Daniel, Moses and a host of others. These manifested the new life in the old.

In our quest to be true disciples of Christ, let us draw life from these notable figures.

*For whatever things were written before were written for our learning, that we through the patience and comfort of the Scriptures might have hope*

*(Rom 15:4).*

Chapter

# THE LAW OF
# EXEMPTION

Text: **For he has put all thing s under his feet. But
when he says "All thing s are put under him," it is
evident that He who put all thing s under Him is
excepted (1 Cor. 15:27).**

As we gradually draw this discourse to a close, our
hearts by now are yearning to get answers to many
questions:

*How then do I deal with my enemies?*

*How do I handle those who hate me?*

*Should I just watch them destroy me in the name of
loving them?*

We are set to answer these questions comprehensively in the
next and last chapter, but first we need to further understand
God's sovereignty over the affairs of men to appreciate why

84

we need to trust Him alone for judgment, fairness and justice. I believe a man will only submit to God's divine orders in handling his enemies when he absolutely trusts Him to be a fair judge.

Hear Him again:

> *Thus says the LORD:" Let not the wise man glory in his wisdom, let not the mighty man glory in his might, nor let the rich man glory in his riches; But let him who glories glory in this, that he understands and knows me, that I am the LORD exercising lovingkindness, judgment and righteousness in the earth, for in these things I delight" says the LORD (Jer. 9:23-24).*

**Why would God say, "Thou shall not kill" and then gleefully introduces Himself as a killer?**

Our God delights in executing lovingkindness, judgment and righteousness on earth. He is a just judge and we must obey Him and also trust Him to defend and fight for us in His own way.

## God Says: "I am a Killer"

Why would God say, *"Thou shall not kill"* and then gleefully introduces Himself as a killer? How would God justifiably do what He says we should not do?

Again, hear Him:

*Now see that I, even I, am He, and there is no God besides Me; I kill and I make alive; I wound and I heal; Nor is there any who can deliver from my hand. For I raise my hand to heaven and say, "I live forever" (Deut. 32:39-40).*

Here we go. God says you and I must not kill, but He says He kills. He can as well wound while you and I are forbidden to wound others. In fact, He says when He decides to deal with an individual; no one can deliver such from His hand. He is God the final judge. While we are mortal, He is immortal. He is above the laws He made, and He is not subject to them. He is the all-knowing God, the creator of the entire universe. Being a just, holy and true God, He alone can mete out justice for the believer in fairness. Therefore, he wants judgment left to Him.

There is a law I wish to call *The Law of Exemption*: the law that exempts the lawgiver and puts him above the law he made. Men also make laws for specific purposes without being bound by them. When they break such laws, it cannot be termed unfairness or injustice. To explain this law, I will be using the following scenarios.

## Scenario 1: The Business Owner

A business owner demands punctuality from his staff. He fixes resumption for 8.00 a.m. every working day and promises to punish severely all erring staff. He strolls in at 2.00 pm and the first thing he reaches out for is the attendance register. Seeing some staff came well after 8.00a.m, he calls on the Manager to issue them queries and punish them according to stipulated rules. Since he came in at 2.00pm, what audacity does he have to punish any erring staff? He made a law he failed to obey. Can anyone accuse him of not keeping to time himself? Would anyone say *"Boss, why would you stroll in at 2.00pm and then punish those who came in just a few minutes past 8.00am?"* No sane man would do that. You see, *he owns their time, they don't own his.* He made the rule but he is exempted from it, and he is not being unfair. Or is he? Definitely not. It's the law of exemption.

## Scenario 2: The Banker's Phone

This may be strange to many, but it is the norm in recent times. In many banks across Nigeria, West Africa, customers are not allowed, for security reasons, to use their mobile phones in the banking hall. There is a notice at the entrance requesting all mobile phones to be switched off. However, customers enter the banking hall, only to see the bank staff themselves using their mobile phones without restraint. Are they above the law? Why would they set a rule for customers and not be bound by it themselves? Simple! It's the law of exemption. Are they wrong? No. Neither do customers feel they are being unfairly treated. The rule is for customers, not members of staff.

An interesting episode happened to me one day at work. While I was having a dialogue on my mobile phone, I spotted a customer afar off, in the banking hall, also making a call. I walked briskly to him, and politely gestured to him to put off his phone while I was still busy using mine. He stopped his conversation abruptly, quickly put off his phone and apologised profusely despite seeing mine still glued to my left ear. He neither felt cheated nor discriminated against. Nor did he accuse me of wrong doing. It's the law of exemption. The law that puts me above the law enacted.

In the same vein, God owns every one of His creation, including you and me. He made us, and the clay cannot say to the potter "What are you trying to do with me?" No one can question His authority. He alone can be fair in meting out justice on earth, and He says Vengeance is mine. Leave it to me. Do not take the laws into your hands. I am the lawgiver. I will be just.

Read again our opening text, 1 Corinthians 15:27. When the Father declared He has put *all* things under the feet of His Son Jesus, the scripture says, though He said ALL, it excluded Him. He is exempted. He is not also under the feet of Jesus. This is understandable. It's the law of exemption.

## Pharaoh and Joseph

When Pharaoh handed over the reins of power of the entire nation of Egypt to Joseph, he obviously exempted himself.

*Then Pharaoh said to Joseph, "In as much as God has shown you all this, there is no one as discerning and as wise as you. You shall be over my house, and all my people shall be ruled according to your word; only in regard to the throne will I be greater than you"* (Gen 41:39-40).

Joseph ruled all of Egypt, and everyone *bowed the knee*, but not Pharaoh. God also does whatever pleases him and remains the righteous judge. The Bible says, *With the merciful You will show Yourself merciful; With a blameless man You will show Yourself blameless; With the pure You will show Yourself pure; And with the devious You will show Yourself shrewd (Psalms18:25-26).* God wants to be the Judge; He only can repay everyone according to their works.

## The Preacher's Eyes

Have you ever attended a church service where the preacher, in closing his sermon, says: "Shall we pray, *all eyes* closed"? The congregation obeys. But then you hear the preacher say "I still see some people looking around. Let's *all* close our eyes, please". The question is: If ALL eyes were closed in the first place, how did the preacher see the roaming eyes? It simply connotes the preacher's eyes were exempted.

**The question is: If ALL eyes were closed in the first place, how did the preacher see the roaming eyes?**

Did he lie to the congregants while he kept his own eyes wide open? No. It is allowed by the law of exemption.

## A Police Chase

I am in love with crime documentaries. You would think it is mostly police chasing bad guys but there is much more that is fascinating. I have watched great documentaries of how police cars were in hot pursuit of men who exceeded speed limit signs. The sign says 80 miles per hour; a driver flagrantly defiles this rule and dangerously goes at 120 miles per hour. In no time, a police car goes after him, flashes at him to stop; he refuses and speeds on, in a bid to escape the law. They pursue hard after him, and in a bid to catch up with him move at speed greater than his, far exceeding the 80 miles limit themselves. They catch up with the erring driver and handcuff him. But in their hot chase, they also have broken the same speed limit and fail to handcuff themselves. Are they unfair? Have they done any wrong? No. They have not. In trying to enforce a law, they are made to break the very law for which they were seeking another's arrest, and are adjudged guiltless. These are interesting aspects of justice and law enforcement. And we are all okay with it.

> **In trying to enforce a law, they are made to break the very law for which they were seeking another's arrest, and are adjudged guiltless.**

Sometimes when a murderer is killed in action, it is just: the murderer's action a crime, the killing of the murderer, a feat. In both cases, blood was shed and lives were snuffed out, but one is unjust and the other, a commendable act.

I am sure you got my drift. Let me explain it further, though. That God the creator can and will also judge man that He has made, meting out severe punishment to them who refuse to repent and He'll be justified to do so. If man can do it justifiably, how much more God! Now we can understand better why Apostle Paul wrote these startling words:

*Since it is a righteous thing with God to repay tribulation to those who trouble you (2 Thess. 1:6).*

God has promised to bring judgment and tribulation to them that trouble you and He is delighted to do it, but He wants you to leave it completely to Him to do, in His own way, at His own time because only Him is exempted from error. He doesn't want you to take the laws into your hands. What will provoke Him to fight for you is when, rather than avenge yourself, you show love to them that hate and trouble you. That's the rule. Play your role, God says. Leave me to play mine. When your enemy is hungry, God says, give him food and ensure he does not go to bed hungry. When I see that, I will fight on your behalf. But when you have abused  him, cursed him, laughed at him and prayed that the hunger should kill him, you have avenged yourself, making yourself no different from him.

**When your enemy is hungry, God says, give him food and ensure he does not go to bed hungry. When I see that, I will fight on your behalf.**

God will not be able to act justifiably on your behalf. As a matter of fact, for your rejoicing, God will let him off the hook. You don't believe that? Here is His word:

*Do not rejoice when your enemy falls, and do not let your heart be glad when he stumbles; Lest the Lord see it, and it displease him, and he turn away His wrath from him (Prov. 24:17-18).*

*If your enemy is hungry, feed him; if he is thirsty, give him a drink; for in so doing you will heap coals of fire on his head. Be not overcome of evil, but overcome evil with good (Romans 12:20-21).*

If only people know it works in the reverse way, they will stop judgemental prayers forthwith, take God's own position and obey him rather than men, and watch Him heap out coals of fire on their enemies.

**Don't repay evil with evil, stop spitting *fire for fire* against supposed human enemies. Spit fire against Satan and his demons. There is a big difference between the two.**

If you truly want God to deal with your enemies, just obey God, follow His word, not the doctrines of men. Follow those who through faith and patience inherit the promises.

Don't repay evil with evil, stop spitting fire for fire against supposed human enemies. Spit fire against Satan and his demons. There is a big difference between the two.

## Soccer to the Rescue

Jesus said, *"If I told you earthly things and you do not believe, how will you believe if I tell you heavenly things?"* (John 3:12). Let's take a final earthly example to explain this divine concept.

The world's greatest sport today is Soccer, also called Football. Okay, I know that may sound partial to a golf fan. And if you follow Cricket or if the Wimbledon Open is your favourite sporting event, you will certainly contest my statement. The fact, however, is that statistics show that the game of soccer has over a billion followers across the globe and rakes in more money than most sports.

While the business of the game may be appealing at some other times, I am interested now in how the rules of the game can be used to explain this important discussion on praying love-fuelled prayers for our enemies.

The soccer pitch is the battle ground of *hostilities* between two equally star-studded teams. The rivalry is real, and in some cases, historical. Think of the *El-classico* between FC Real Madrid and FC Barcelona in the Spanish league, or the Manchester *derby* between Manchester United and Manchester City in the English Premiership.

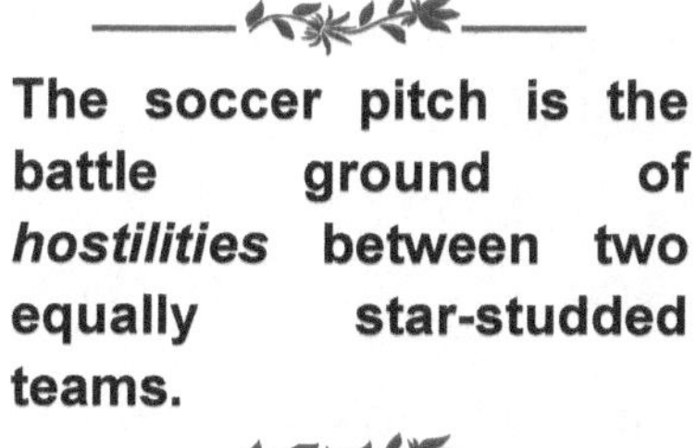

**The soccer pitch is the battle ground of *hostilities* between two equally star-studded teams.**

The sheer passion, the mammoth crowd of die-hard fans on both sides, like as it were, *cloud of witnesses*. The mind games, the pre-match predictions and a whole gamut of stuff.

Despite the high stakes, it is never a do-or-die affair not for the players, nor for the coaches, neither is it for the fans. On the field of play, there are *rules of engagement*. There is a centre referee who enforces rules, ensures justice and fairness while the game lasts. Without them, competitive games are meaningless.

If I may call him that, the centre referee is the *god* of the match.

Put in layman's language, a rule of the football game says in essence, *"In the event that you (a player) are badly tackled, deliberately and severely by your opponent, which requires justice and fairness, do not retaliate by yourself. Vengeance is the referee's, who will issue a red card or yellow card, depending on the nature or severity of the offence. Any player who retaliates and takes the law into his own hands shall suffer the same fate as the offending player."*

Is this not both interesting and scriptural?

**Friends, so are the issues of the kingdom of God. Unlike these players, we do not deceive the Umpire of the universe to get his attention.**

This is fantastic and can help us articulate some more points. So, we have a player badly tackled by the opponent. He gets up and angrily charges at the offender, hitting him in the face in retaliation. The referee brings out the red card, flashes it, first to the offender and equally to the offended. Both depart the field of play, thereby depleting the strength of their teams.

The offender is foolish for injuring another player, but the greater fool is the offended who did not leave vengeance to the referee, but allowed himself to be sent off.

An offended player only needs to be wise and exercise self-control. Some players understand this. Instead of rising to fight for themselves, they rather hold on to their injured legs, roll violently on the turf, screaming dramatically for attention. Some do this even when not in pain to get the referee on their side. They want him to do the needful: pull out a red card and end it for the player, giving your own team a numerical edge, and yourself the opportunity to carry on in the field of play.

Friends, so are the issues of the kingdom of God.

Unlike these players, we do not deceive the Umpire of the universe to get his attention. His eyes are overall and we only need to allow him to do what He does best: judge rightly.

But he does require us to be mindful of these words of Peter:

*Finally, all of you be of one mind, having compassion for one another; love as brothers, be tender hearted, be courteous; not returning evil for evil or reviling for reviling, but on the contrary blessing, knowing that you were called to this, that you may inherit a blessing. For "He who will love life, and see good days, let him refrain his tongue from evil, and his lips from speaking deceit. Let him turn away from evil and do good; let him seek peace and pursue it. For the eyes of the Lord are on the righteous, and His ears are open to their prayers; But the face of the Lord is against those who do evil" (1 Pet 3:8-12).*

Do you know how Peter rounds off this argument? Let's see it from the Bible again: **And who is he who will harm you if you become followers of what is good?** (1 Pet 3:13, emphasis mine).

Wow, what a promise!

**Have you not seen referees during football matches miss obvious infringements, all because when it happened their eyes were fixed on other spots on the field?**

He promised that no one will be able to harm you, but on the condition that you also follow what is good. That God says you should love your enemies does not make Him overlook their evil. *I will avenge*, he says. And only the all-knowing God can judge righteously.

Have you not seen referees during football matches miss obvious infringements, all because when it happened their eyes were fixed on other spots on the field? Little wonder he has Assistants who are his eyes for areas his limited eyes cannot cover. He trusts them absolutely to know an *offside play* for example. The game would have lost its shine if offside goals are made to count. And in some cases, it is so because they are all limited. But God is exempted from error. He not only sees clearly all things, He also knows the motives behind every action. The Bible says: *"He who planted the ear, shall he not hear? He who formed the eye, shall he not see?"(Ps. 94:9).*

# God the Judge

Does it not appeal to our sense of justice and fairness when a rapist murderer is put behind bars for the rest of his life with hard labour or sent to the hangman? When society judges that a man is too dangerous to live among decent humans,

have they infringed on his fundamental human right to enjoy freedom of movement and action? Would you not rather feel a sense of injustice if such is let go in spite of damning evidences? Won't you scream blue murder? Should it then be difficult to understand God's word on issues of eternity?

Listen; there is a coming kingdom, and a soon-coming King. In this kingdom dwells only righteousness. Then, God has determined to lock out every unrighteousness in hell, with Satan, the father of all unrighteousness. Why should this be difficult to understand? In Football, FIFA sets the rules, not the players. On the earth and for this kingdom, God sets the rules, not you and me. Why would a player set his own rules and think he can go far in the game? No. He accepts and adapts.

**Listen; there is a coming kingdom, and a soon-coming King.**

We can only enter God's kingdom on God's own terms, not ours. Good enough, God's rules have been set out clearly in His word.

Please take time to read with me: 2 Peter 3:8-14

*8. But beloved, do not forget this one thing, that with the Lord one day is as a thousand years, and a thousand years as one day.*

*9. The Lord is not slack concerning His promise as some count slackness, but is longsuffering toward us, not willing that any should perish but that all should come to repentance.*

*10. But the day of the Lord will come as a thief in the night, in which the heavens will pass away with a great noise, and the elements will melt with fervent heat; both the earth and the works that are in it will be burned up.*

*11. Therefore, since all these things will be dissolved, what manner of persons ought ye to be in holy conduct and godliness.*

*12. Looking for and hastening the coming of the day of God, because of which the heavens will be dissolved, being on fire, and all the elements will melt with fervent heat?*

*13. **Nevertheless we, according to His promise, look for new heavens and a new earth in which righteousness dwells.***

*14. Therefore beloved, looking forward to these things, be diligent to be found by Him in peace, without spot, and blameless. (emphasis mine)*

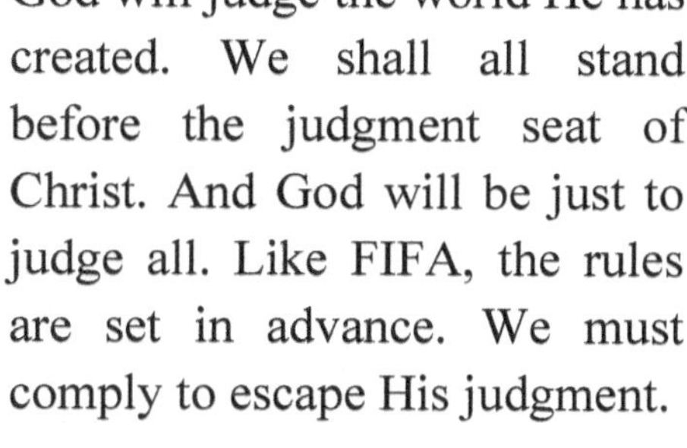

**God will judge the world He has created. We shall all stand before the judgment seat of Christ. And God will be just to judge all. Like FIFA, the rules are set in advance. We must comply to escape His judgment.**

God will judge the world He has created. We shall all stand before the judgment seat of Christ. And God will be just to judge all. Like FIFA, the rules are set in advance. We must comply to escape His judgment.

God will judge the world He has created. We shall all stand before the judgment seat of Christ. And God will be just to judge all. Like FIFA, the rules are set in advance. We must comply to escape His judgment.

Chapter

# DEALING WITH YOUR
# ENEMIES

## Throwback from Paul's Diary

In the first chapter of this book, Paul's journal revealed to us his experiences in a Philippian jail and his handling of the jailer. We have emphasized that, more often than not, we fight the wrong enemy and this has made us ineffective in the place of prayer. We really have only one enemy, Satan and his cohorts. We should therefore aim our arsenals at the source of our challenges or we may not get lasting results.

We may ask ourselves this question: Who truly was Paul's enemy in the events that played out in the book of Acts Chapter 16? Was it the jailer or the magistrates who ordered that he and Silas be remanded in prison? We were told that it was the magistrates that actually ordered their beating and the prison remand (See Acts 16:22-23). Had Paul allowed the jailer to die, would the jailer's death automatically bring freedom to him? I don't think so. The jailer was simply acting on instructions, carrying out the directives of his superiors.

**Until the magistrates asked the jailer to release them, Paul and Silas would not have been free men even if the jailer died; that is if they are not accused of complicity in the death of the jailer, further prolonging their stay.**

Until the magistrates asked the jailer to release them, Paul and Silas would not have been free men even if the jailer died; that is if they are not accused of complicity in the death of the jailer, further prolonging their stay.

*And when it was day, the magistrates sent the officers saying, 'Let those men go'. So the keeper of the prison reported these words to Paul saying, 'The magistrates have sent to let you go. Now therefore depart and go in peace' (Acts 16:35-36).* That's how it works. The source of Paul's travails was not the Jailer; his death might not have made any difference to their captivity.

In this final chapter, could you allow me offer some final examples from the Bible and then I will close with a personal narrative from my days at the university.

## QUEEN ESTHER

Another character in scriptures who understood how spiritual warfare works was Esther. A decree was signed by the king Ahasuerus to eliminate all Jews in Medes and Persia, orchestrated by a Jew hater, Haman. In Medes and Persia, the law was superior to the king. Once the king signs it, the king cannot alter it. (Remember Daniel and king Darius. It was under Medes and Persian rule). Had Haman succeeded, he would have been the first Hitler.

Thank God for Mordecai, Esther's adopted father, who understood how it works. Mordecai and Esther knew the focus was not Haman but the satanic forces operating in high places working to annihilate the Jews but were merely using Haman as a front. They therefore took the battle to the gates of the real enemy, declaring a 3-day absolute fast-no food, no water- to change a decree that is humanly impossible to change. They quenched the raging fire in the spirit realm, standing on God's numerous promises to their fathers, and making their own heavenly decrees. The Bible says, *"Thou shall also decree a thing and it shall be established unto thee..." (Job 22:28 KJV)*. They got victory in the spirit realm and the rest was formality. Mordecai understood that Jews were God's covenant race and their lives and continued existence cannot be in the hands of a human enemy called Haman.

**Mordecai and Esther knew the focus was not Haman but the satanic forces operating in high places working to annihilate the Jews but were merely using Haman as a front.**

Even when Haman had got the king to sign the decree, Mordecai still refused to bow to him. He was audacious. It's like saying *"This issue has been taken beyond you, Haman. I have no direct business with you."* He recognized who the true enemy was and they had dealt him a fatal blow in the spirit. The rest was formality. And so it was; the situation was reversed; Haman who received the bow from everyone was the same man who drove Mordecai round town proclaiming before him that everyone should bow the knee to him. (See Esther Chapter 6). This is however not our focus. There is a more crucial issue to note.

## A Banquet Just for Three

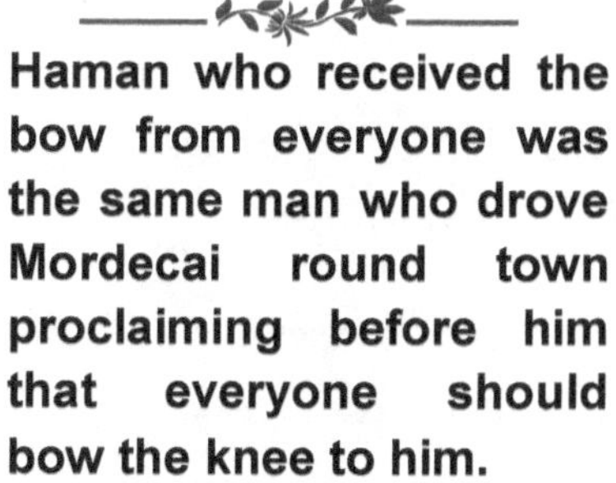

**Haman who received the bow from everyone was the same man who drove Mordecai round town proclaiming before him that everyone should bow the knee to him.**

By divine wisdom, Esther had invited the king and Haman to a private banquet. A banquet just for three. The king, having noticed the queen was bothered about some issues, asked her for the third time to make her request, any request, and it will be granted, even if to relinquish half his kingdom to her.

That was favour, God had gone ahead to make crooked paths straight. Esther presented the matter bothering her to the king. Someone, she said, was plotting to personally destroy her and her people. The king could not believe it and he requested to know who could plot against his queen. Esther then revealed that the wicked plotter was this very Haman, the third person at the banquet. The impact of the news on the king was total; he ordered that Haman be hanged immediately. God was at work.

*Then Queen Esther answered and said, "If I have found favor in your sight, O king, and if it pleases the king, let my life be given me at my petition, and my people at my request.*

*For we have been sold, my people and I, to be destroyed, to be killed, and to be annihilated. Had we been sold as male and female slaves, I would have held my tongue, although the enemy could never compensate for the king's loss"*

*So king Ahasuerus answered and said to Queen Esther, "Who is he, and where is he, who would dare presume in his heart to do such a thing?"*

*And Esther said, "The adversary and enemy is this wicked Haman!" So Haman was terrified before the king and queen (Esther 7:3-6).*

In fury, the king ordered Haman to be hanged on the gallows he had earlier prepared for Mordecai (See Esther 7:9).

**It is worthy of note however, that it was not Esther who requested that the king should kill Haman. She only reported him to the king, and God the righteous judge took it on from there.**

It is worthy of note however, that it was not Esther who requested that the king should kill Haman. She only reported him to the king, and God the righteous judge took it on from there. This is what we have said over and over. Let's leave judgment to God. She did not ask for it, but God did it. Esther understood how it works and we should as well.

More importantly, Esther also understood that the death of Haman changed nothing. An unchangeable decree subsists still; all Jews would still die on the thirteenth day of December of that year. Her goal was to get the decree repealed, not to get Haman killed, and a decree had never been repealed in the history of Medes and Persia. This is where we miss it. Were it to be in our days, on the death of Haman, many would take to the streets rejoicing, sharing testimonies in Church, yet a time bomb is still ticking. Thank God Esther knew that the hanging of Haman and his 10 sons hasn't changed anything. They could be alive for all she cares; the crucial issue is repealing an irrevocable decree.

See how she pushed for repeal in spite of the odds:

*Now Esther spoke again to the king, fell down at his feet, and implored him with tears to counteract the evil of Haman the Agagite, and the scheme which he devised against the Jews.*

*And the king held out the golden scepter toward Esther. So Esther arose and stood before the king, and said, "If it pleases the king, and if I have found favor in his sight and the thing seems right to the king and I am pleasing in his eyes, let it be written to revoke the letters devised by Haman, the son of Hammedatha the Agagite, which he wrote to annihilate the Jews who are in all the king's provinces. For how can I endure to see the evil that will come to my people? Or how can I endure to see the destruction of my countrymen?" (Esther 8:3-6).*

> **This mission must not fail. A time bomb was ticking, waiting to explode on a set date. Even though the bomber has been arrested and killed, until this bomb is detonated, destruction will still visit the Jews on an unprecedented scale, and even the king will not be able to save the queen.**

Rather than run around rejoicing that Haman was dead and sharing testimonies, look at what she did. She fell at the king's feet, she cried, she wept, she pleaded. She knew the enormity of what was at stake. This mission must not fail. A time bomb was ticking, waiting to explode on a set date. Even though the bomber has been arrested and killed, until this bomb is detonated, destruction will still visit the Jews on an unprecedented scale, and even the king will not be able to save the queen.

And so, she sought the reversal of the decree. It has never happened before, yes, but they are Jews, children of a covenant-keeping God. They have prayed and He promised to hear them in the day of trouble. And He did. Hallelujah!

*Then King Ahasuerus said to Queen Esther and Mordecai the Jew, "Indeed, I have given Esther the house of Haman, and they have hanged him on the gallows because he tried to lay his hands on the Jews, You yourselves write a decree concerning the Jews, as you please, in the king's name, and seal it with the king's signet ring; for whatever is written in the king's signet ring no man can revoke" (Esther 8:7-8). Hallelujah!*

The king could not actually revoke the earlier decree; the law does not allow it. He only signed another decree which superseded the earlier one. God fought for His people. On the said date, the 13th day of December, rather than the Jews dying, it was their enemies that died. Then and only then did the celebration begin. It was an unprecedented turnaround for the Jews. Two scriptures aptly capture the entire episode.

Esther 4:3

*And in every province where the king's command and decree (first decree) arrived, **there was great mourning among the Jews, with fasting, weeping and wailing; and many lay in sackcloth and ashes** (emphasis mine).*

Esther 8:17

*And in every province and city, wherever the king's command and decree came (second decree), **the Jews had joy and gladness, a feast and a holiday.** Then many of the people of the land became Jews, because the fear of Jews fell upon them (Emphasis mine).*

I repeat: Focus on the source of the challenge, which is the devil, the rest is formality. But when you focus on demolishing, cursing and praying against human agents, victory does not last. The enemy can easily replace them. In football, if a player is injured, the team replaces him.

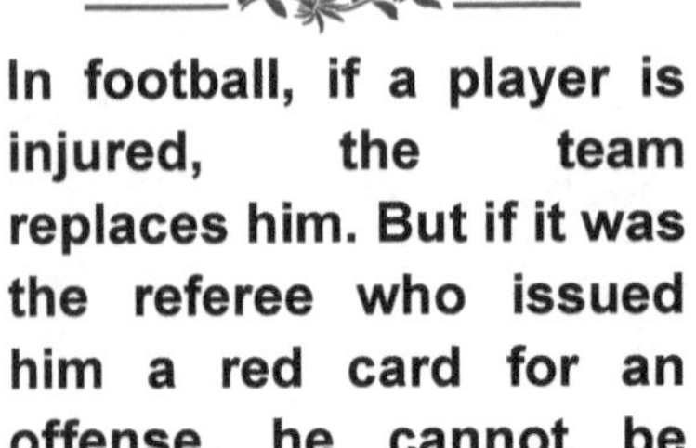

> In football, if a player is injured, the team replaces him. But if it was the referee who issued him a red card for an offense, he cannot be replaced. God is the referee in the game of life.

But if it was the referee who issued him a red card for an offense, he cannot be replaced. God is the referee in the game of life. Pluck off a leaf, another grows in its place, uproot the tree, nothing else can grow. We wrestle not against flesh and blood.

## Like Haman, Like Ahitophel

Just like God overturned Haman's murderous plan, the story of David and Ahitophel shows what happens when God defeats the counsel of friends who hurt us or stab us in the back.

When Absalom, David's son overthrew his father and the latter ran for his life, Ahitophel, his right hand man and counsellor, decided to stay back and team up with the rebel. When David was told about the betrayal of his trusted adviser, he prayed a prayer that was decisive in restoring the throne back to him.

*Then someone told David, saying, "Ahitophel is among the conspirators with Absalom." And David said, "O LORD, I pray, turn the counsel of Ahitophel into foolishness!" (2 Samuel 15:31).*

**Please note that, just like Esther, David did not ask God to kill Ahitophel. He only asked that Absalom would not heed the very good advice that might come from Ahitophel.**

Please note that, just like Esther, David did not ask God to kill Ahitophel. He only asked that Absalom would not heed the very good advice that might come from Ahitophel. And God answered. Absalom refused the good counsel from Ahitophel.

*So Absalom and all the men of Israel said, "The advice of Hushai the Archite is better than the advice of Ahitophel." For the LORD had purposed to defeat the good advice of Ahitophel, to the intent that the LORD might bring disaster on Absalom*

*(2 Samual 17:14).*

*What then happened? Now when Ahithophel saw that his advice was not followed, he saddled a donkey, and arose and went home to his house, to his city. Then he put his household in order, and hanged himself, and died; and he was buried in his father's tomb*

*(2 Samuel 17:23).*

Can you see that David did not ask God to kill Ahitophel, but God ensured a *friend-turned-enemy* of David's never survived his rebellion against the anointed?

This is how it should be in spiritual warfare. Don't ask for the death of your enemy. Deal with the forces at work in them; frustrate all their efforts against you and leave God to decide how he wants to judge the matter.

**This is how it should be in spiritual warfare. Don't ask for the death of your enemy. Deal with the forces at work in them**

## A Personal Testimony

In my final year in college, I had a lecturer who one day in his office told me point blank that he would not allow me to graduate that year. He was dead serious. As he was my supervisor, I courteously told him I would. When he asked how sure I was, I bravely reached out for my bag and brought out my Bible to read some scriptures to him. That got him annoyed. He lashed out, "You want to preach to me? Am I not your supervisor? Let's see how you will graduate from this university".

From that moment on, he deliberately frustrated my work, unnecessarily cancelling all my write ups and would ask me to start all over again. Halfway into my project he cancelled the topic. Having gone to the field for research, he insisted

**Halfway into my project he cancelled the topic. Having gone to the field for research, he insisted I did not. When my colleagues were rounding off, I was still struggling to start.**

I did not. When my colleagues were rounding off, I was still struggling to start. Time was obviously running out as final semester exams approached. At some point, except a miracle happened, I knew I could not finish. I recognized that this definitely was the devil's handiwork and that I might not graduate with my colleagues. It was a major battle but I was certain it was the kind of battle my Father specializes in. God is Jehovah the man of war Himself.

In the light of our discourse, my supervisor is surely an enemy. He wants to block my progress and advancement for no just cause. Should my supervisor not "die by fire"? Not at all! I knew I was not wrestling against flesh and blood. He wasn't the true enemy. He was just a pawn in a chess game. A power was at work through him to work against me. It's that power I had business with.

> **I took the battle to the gates of the enemy in warfare, destroying all the strongholds of the enemy working through him.**

I took the battle to the gates of the enemy in warfare, destroying all the strongholds of the enemy working through him. Through incessant intercession, fasting, and praying in the spirit, I persevered until I had a breakthrough in my spirit that the answer had come. I asked that other brethren join me in the fight. We are to bear one another's burden, after all.

On a particular day, I entered his office and he invited me to sit down. I was surprised. He then started a conversation. I noticed he was calm and sober. He then asked if I knew every human being is related to each other one way or the other. I replied in the negative. He said if he begins to inquire into my background, I would be surprised that there would be a link somewhere between us. It could be my uncle was his classmate in his college days abroad or something. He then cited an instance of when he met a total stranger, only to find out the man was a relation of his friend. Then he smiled and said, "So why don't we love each other? We are all brothers and sisters. Somehow we are all related". I listened with total disbelief. "Could this be the same man", I seemed to ask myself. All said and done, he then asked me to drop my work, the chapters I had written for him to read. I was shocked but thanked him and left his office in amazement.

**The student he promised would not graduate wrote the best project for him that year.**

A few days later, a fellow student he also supervises called me and said he was in his office and the supervisor asked him to read my work, that it's the best project of the six students he was supervising that year. The rest is history. The student he promised would not graduate wrote the best project for him that year. The man is still alive today, and I learnt he later gave his life to Christ. I am grateful to God I did not send him to an early grave simply because he boasted that I would not graduate. The Bible says *"The king's heart is in the hand of the LORD, like rivers of water; He turns it wherever He wishes (Prov. 21:1).*Through proper warfare, the same man changed and adjudged me his best student and also surrendered to Christ. That's what the power of God can do.

Our prayers should witness to the love and power of God; not kill perceived enemies.

## Your True Enemy

We cannot over-emphasize the crucial issue which has been at the heart of this book. Christians more often than not are fighting the wrong enemy, and the reason is clear: *We don't seem to be fully aware of the enormity of the forces we are up against in this present world.* Let us therefore remind ourselves of some salient facts:

- *Satan is the god of this world* (2 Cor. 4:4).In this present dispensation, all the systems of the world are under the authority and control of Satan and his cohorts. God did not give him this power and authority, man did. Through disobedience in the Garden of Eden, Adam literally handed over the authority and power God gave him to the devil. When Satan tempted the Lord by showing him all the kingdoms of the world and the glory of it, he boasted *"All this authority I will give you, and their glory; for this has been delivered to me, and I give to whomever I wish"* (Luke 4:6). If he was lying, Jesus would have told him so. Power and authority was truly delivered to him. Who was the transferor? Not God but Adam.

- John says, *"We know that we are of God, and the whole world lies under the sway of the wicked one"* (1 John 5:19). We are God's children operating in enemy territory. We are God's light in gross darkness and the darkness thickens by the day. Events all around us testify to this.

♦ *The thief comes to steal, to kill and to destroy* (John 10:10). *He is the accuser of the brethren* (Rev 12:10). *He walks about seeking whom to devour* (1 Peter 5:8). *He does not like to open the door of his prisoners* (Isaiah 14:17). *He makes the earth to tremble* (Isaiah 14:16).

♦ Jesus the Lord came and by His death on the cross destroyed the works of the devil. *"...For this purpose the Son of God was manifested, that He might destroy the works of the devil"* (1 John 3:8). He took power and authority back from the enemy, *"In as much then as the children have partaken of flesh and blood, He Himself likewise shared in the same, that through death He might destroy him that had the power of death, that is the devil, and release those who through the fear of death were all their lifetime subject to bondage"* (Heb. 2:14-15). He also said, *"I am he who lives, and was dead, and behold, I am alive for evermore, amen; And I have the keys of hell and death"* (Rev. 1:18).

♦ The Lord has handed the authority back to the church and gave us power over the enemy. *"And He said to them, 'I saw Satan fall like lightning from heaven. Behold, I give you the authority to trample on serpents and scorpions, and over all the power of the enemy, and nothing shall by any means hurt you"* (Luke 10:18-19).

♦ We are now to exercise that authority over the forces of darkness as we take our position in Christ. *"...And raised us up together, and made us sit together in the heavenly places in Christ Jesus..."* (Eph. 2:6). The greater one dwells in us *"You are of God, little children, and have overcome them, because He who is in you is greater than he (Satan) who is in the world"* (1 John 4:4). *"...For whatever is born of God overcomes the world. And this is the victory that has overcome the world- our faith."* (1 John 5:4). We are to teach Satan and demons the wisdom of God. *"To the intent that now unto the principalities and powers in heavenly places might be known by the church the manifold wisdom of God (Eph. 3:10).* The word also says, *"And the God of peace will crush Satan under your feet shortly..."* (Rom. 16:20).

♦ Children of God are primarily spirit beings because their spirits have been recreated by the Spirit of God. *"... That which is born of the Spirit is spirit"* (John 3:6). By our spirit we relate to God and the spirit world. The more our spirit grows, the more he gains ascendancy over the flesh. (Romans 8:13).

♦ As spirit beings, we are perpetually a target of the enemy who is sad to lose us to God's kingdom while the heavens rejoiced for gaining us. So, Satan daily engages us in battle to take us back and discourage us while God who has given us His victory expects us to triumph always over the enemy by exercising our God-given authority. *"Now thanks be unto God, which always causeth us to triumph in Christ..."* (2 Cor.2:14 KJV). He also says, *"Yet in all these things we are more than conquerors through Him who loved us"* *(Rom. 8:37).*

♦ Behind virtually every battle that comes our way therefore as Children of God is an orchestrated, well laid out plan by the devil. Many a time it does not look like it, but most times it is so. Even this enemy of ours can appear as angel of light. *"And no wonder! For Satan himself transforms himself into an angel of light"* (2 Cor 11:14). Since he uses human agents and circumstances to fight us, we always don't recognize he is the one behind it. So we tend to focus on the human agents.

♦ *Make no mistake about it.* Satan, the accuser of the brethren works behind the scene most, if not all, of the time. *"For we do not wrestle against flesh and blood, but against principalities, against powers, against the rulers of the darkness of this age, against spiritual hosts of wickedness in the heavenly places"* *(Eph. 6:12).*

♦ What then should we do? *"Therefore take up the whole armor of God, that you may be able to withstand in the evil day, and having done all, to stand (Eph.6:13).*

♦ What are these armours: *"Stand therefore, having guided your waist with Truth, having put on the breastplate of Righteousness, and having shod your feet with the preparation of the Gospel of Peace, above all, taking The Shield of Faith with which to quench all the fiery darts of the wicked one. And take the Helmet of Salvation, and The Sword of the Spirit, which is the Word of God; Praying Always with all prayer and supplication In The Spirit... (Eph.6:13-18).* Recognise it is the wicked one throwing those fiery darts at you and not your boss or your wife or your husband or your lecturer. That's what the scripture above says.

♦ With the weapons of warfare, you defend and attack the enemy at the same time. Your defense weapons are: your helmet (your salvation must be sure), your shield (faith in God), your shoes (readiness to war a good warfare), your belt (proper understanding of God's word), your breastplate (God's righteousness and your righteous living serving as bullet proof against dangerous darts).

♦ The offensive weapons are: The Sword of the Spirit (God's word that is living and active and sharp, coming from your mouth) and Prayers (majorly in the language of the Spirit. Deep must call unto deep). The damage a physical sword will do to a human body is nothing compared to the damage God's word will do to spiritual forces. It is said to be sharper than any man-made double-edged sword.

♦ Praying is largely done in the language of the Spirit. That is where force is matched with force. You don't take a knife to a gunfight. Only the Spirit can search all things and pray with accuracy *"...Likewise the Spirit also helps our weaknesses. For we do not know what we should pray for as we ought, but the Spirit Himself makes intercession for us with groaning which cannot be uttered. Now He who searches the hearts knows what the mind of the Spirit is, because He makes intercession according to the will of God"* (Rom. 8:26-27).

♦ *Fasting is an essential ingredient of spiritual warfare.* Some issues require not just praying, but also fasting, which is denying oneself of legitimate human needs to focus on crucial issues of warfare. It is a way of saying the issue at stake is more crucial than my appetite. Jesus, after casting out a demon says, *Howbeit, this kind goeth not out but by prayer and fasting* (Matt. 17:21 KJV).

♦ *The devil is not fighting alone.* He has a spiritual hierarchy and hosts of demons carrying out his bidding. Don't fight your major battles alone either. There is strength in number... *"Again, I say to you that if two of you agree on earth concerning anything that they ask, it will be done for them by My Father in heaven. For where two or three are gathered together in My name, I am there in the midst of them"* *(Matt.18:19-20)*. You know quite well that one shall chase a thousand and two shall put ten thousand to flight (See Deut. 32:30). By inference three will chase a hundred thousand and four will put a million to flight. *Every individual added puts a zero at the back of the existing number.*

◆ *The mind is the battleground.* The fiery darts are spiritual arrows thrown by the enemy in the form of thoughts, imaginations, arguments contrary to the knowledge of God; lies and evil counsels from the pit of hell. He wants the believer to accept them as his own thoughts, believe them and speak in line with or act on it. With our spiritual weapons, we reject the counsels and lies and machinations of the enemy, hold firm to God's word and push back the forces operating against us. *"For though we walk in the flesh, we do not war according to the flesh. For the weapons of our warfare are not carnal but mighty in God for pulling down strongholds, casting down arguments and every high thing that exalts itself against the knowledge of God, bringing every thought into captivity to the obedience of Christ, and being ready to punish all disobedience when your obedience is fulfilled (2 Cor.10:3-6).*

◆ *The kingdom of God suffers violence, only the violent takes it by force,* says the Lord Himself (Matt. 11:12).

There is no great promise of God for you that the devil will not contest. If it is not contested, there may not be much to it. Therefore, stand firm and *"Do not cast away your confidence which has great reward, for ye have need of endurance, so that after you have done the will of God, you may receive the promise.* (Heb. 10:35-36). Remember that our father Abraham through patient endurance received God's promises. *"And so after he had patiently endured, he obtained the promise"* (Heb. 6:15).

♦ *Bind the Strong Man.* Jesus called Satan a strong man who will not readily give up on his devilish ploys. But He called us the stronger one and gave us authority to bind the devil. *"When a strong man, fully armed, guards his palace, his goods are in peace. But when a stronger than he comes upon him, he takes from him all his armor in which he trusted and divides his spoils"* We are the greater one because the greater One dwells in us. He says, *"And I will give you the keys of the kingdom of heaven, and whatever you bind on earth will be bound in heaven, and whatever you loose on earth shall be loosed in heaven"* (Matt. 16:19).

♦ *Finally, pray without ceasing* (1 Thess. 5:17). *Be fervent and aglow in the spirit* (Rom. 12:11). Only *"the effectual fervent prayers of a righteous man avails much"* (James 5:16). *Be strong in the Lord and in the power of His might* (Eph. 6:10). *Having done all, STAND (Eph. 6:13).*

# EPILOGUE

## *The Secret Place*

Let us be clear. Only God, the sovereign King, decides who dies or not. Praying that our enemies should *fall down and die* is not a reflection of his love and mercy. Our prayers ought to affirm his Lordship and submit to his majestic display of love. A wise Christian leaves vengeance to him. Of course, there are instances when human vessels pay dearly for standing in the way of a child of God and God, the righteous judge decides to visit them with destruction. That is left to God, not a product of selfish and vengeful prayers.

The world of science has given us much to ponder about as it explores God's magnificent world. Since true science is in line with God's word, we can borrow a final thought that helps us understand this issue one last time.

Do you recall your science class on *Newton's Law of Gravity?* The sheer size of the earth makes it attract everything to itself. Whatever goes up must, therefore, come down. We can walk on earth, have objects stay firmly on it because of this law. That much we know.

But then when astronauts go to the moon, we see a different picture. We see them float around in the cabin of the space ship, their legs not touching the ground at all and need not to. They literally walk on air. It's a wonder to see them pour water out of a cup and the water hangs on a spot in the air.

They now propel themselves to float to the spot and "pick" up the water with their mouth. It's fun.

The fun aside, why do they float? How did they defy the law of gravity in space? Let me offer one possible answer.

They have become so far away from planet earth where the Law of Gravity exists and for them, by sheer distance, the law no longer holds for them. So, what to us on earth is a miracle is natural to them. As a matter of fact, for them to be able to walk on the moon, they need to create *"artificial gravity"* just to be able to keep their feet on the moon surface. That's why we see them drag their feet. Without that weight tied to their feet, they would float away and possibly perish.

Why is this science topic important? I believe there is available in God a level and depth that suspends the elements others are subject to. There is a realm of the spiritual to which we have been called to operate as sons of God. This realm is devoid of natural laws.

This is a level we all need to aspire to, if only because, at this divine terrain, you do not need to bother about any kind of enemy.

This spiritual realm is a place where you are untouchable, and are so insulated you care less about an enemy.

This realm is called the Secret Place of the Most High. Here is how the Psalms describe it:

*He who dwells in the secret place of the Most High shall abide under the shadow of the Almighty. I will say of the Lord, "He is my refuge and my fortress: My God, in Him I will trust." Surely, He shall deliver you from the snare of the fowler and from the perilous pestilence. He shall cover you with His feathers, and under His wings you shall take refuge; His truth shall be your shield and buckler. You shall not be afraid of the terror by night, nor of the arrow that flies by day, nor of the pestilence that walks in darkness, nor of the destruction that lays waste at noonday. A thousand may fall at your side, and ten thousand at your right hand; but it shall not come near you. Only with your eyes shall you look, and see the reward of the wicked. Because you have made the LORD, who is my refuge, even the Most High your dwelling place, No evil shall befall you, nor shall any plague come near your dwelling... (Psalm 91: 1-10).*

Can you imagine these exceedingly great and precious promises in God's word? A place where sicknesses and affliction can't reach you. You can even trample upon lions and serpents and they hide to avoid you. May we all find our place there.

Interestingly, some go in there occasionally but those who are smart dwell there as permanent residents.

Since it's the permanent residing we are talking about, David, that OT saint with the new dispensation mindset seemed to have understood it. Here are his words in Ps 27: *That I may dwell in the house of the Lord ALL THE DAYS of my life....* (4, emphasis mine). I like this translation of the verse: *The one thing I want from God, the thing I seek most of all, is the privilege of meditating in his Temple, living in his presence every day of my life, delighting in his incomparable perfections and glory* (Psalm 27: 4, The Living Bible).

This Patriarch knew something we still don't know. Even as he fought God's wars, he knew where his true dwelling place is. No wonder he won all his battles and died peacefully.

And when he lost that presence through sin and carelessness, he cried out for it.

As I conclude this book, I want to thank you for giving me your time; and I also would like to share this prayer with you: That we may both dwell in His secret place to behold His beauty every day of our lives.

> And as we do, Ps 114 is fulfilled in us. *"When Israel went out of Egypt, the house of Jacob from a people of strange language, Judah became His sanctuary, And Israel His dominion. The sea saw it and fled; Jordan turned back (1-3).*

The enemies see something we don't see and take to their heels. The mountains, hills, great waters see something that you and I are not even conscious of and you wonder why they run. Could it be because of the point David makes in one of the closing verses of that same chapter?

*Tremble, O earth, at the presence of the Lord, At the presence of the God of Jacob (7).*

Here is David's answer to why the enemy has raced from him: the presence of the God of Jacob with his people. This is all that is important for the Christian; the practice of the presence of God. Rather than focus on the enemy, it is what we ought to passionately crave.

God's church will get there surely, and the gates of hell will not be able to prevail against us. Those who try to harm us end up harming themselves; sometimes, without our knowledge. And when we get to know, we won't hate or curse them. We realize, as James notes that "no stream brings forth sweet and bitter at the same time" (3:11). We are not such Christians.

We curse not. We bless, telling them to come unto Him who paid a price for them and to be reconciled to GOD

We curse not. We bless, telling them: ***Do yourself no harm!***